I0456486

Living Into
the Truth

Living Into the Truth

A Daughter's Journey of Discovery

Annette Marquis

WordsWomen

WWP
p r e s s

Richmond, Virginia

WordsWomen Press

An Imprint of WordsWomen Enterprises, LLC

Richmond, Virginia, USA

Author's note: Some names and identifying characteristics have been changed to protect the identities of the people I wrote about. In some cases, time has been compressed and dialogue approximated. The events are as true to my memory as possible. Although many major life events are included, others have been intentionally left out to maintain the focus on this story.

LIBRARY OF CONGRESS CATALOGING-IN-PUBLICATION DATA

Names: Marquis, Annette, 1955-author. Title: Living into the truth : a daughter's journey of discovery / Annette Marquis.

Description: Richmond, VA: WordsWomen Press, 2024.

Identifiers: ISBN 979-8-9912802-2-8 (hardcover) | ISBN 979-8-9912802-0-4 (paperback) | ISBN 979-8-9912802-1-1 (ebook) | ISBN 979-8-9912802-3-5 (audiobook)

Subjects: LCSH: Women--Biography. | Lesbians--Biography. | LGBTQ+ people--Biography. | Genetic Testing--Personal Narratives. | Family secrets. | Autobiography. | BISAC: BIOGRAPHY & AUTOBIOGRAPHY / LGBTQ+| BIOGRAPHY & AUTOBIOGRAPHY / Women. | BIOGRAPHY & AUTOBIOGRAPHY / Memoirs.

Classification: LCCHQ75.3 .L582024 (print) | LCCHQ75.3 (ebook) | DDC306.76 /63--dc23.

Book Cover by Phillip Hilliker | Photos by Annette Marquis and Nancy Pierce Photo

For Wendy,
My inspiration, motivation, and the joy of my life
&
for Sidney Abbot and Barbara Love,
authors of
Sappho was a Right-On Woman: A Liberated View of Lesbianism,
the book that opened my heart and eyes
and helped me become who I am

Contents

Prologue

LETTERS TO MY MOTHER

Letter 1

D ear Mom,

   You've been gone more than twenty years now, and I still think of you every day. Most days, I wish I could call to catch up on our daily lives like we used to. I loved the way you could laugh at yourself and the situations you found yourself in—like the time you picked up the wrong line while working in the Sears Roebuck catalog department. Thinking you were talking to a woman about fencing, instead you asked a woman ordering bras if she wanted the kind that "stretched all the way around her property."

   Remember how you couldn't stop laughing that day? I can still picture the yellow telephone hanging on the kitchen wall with the long yellow cord stretching all the way to my bedroom.

I remember calling you at work that day when all you could do was stammer. "C-c-call, call you back," you finally spit out, words punctuated by guffaws and shallow breathing. We laughed about that story for years.

I still see you riding the cable cars in San Francisco, and I can feel my anxiety as I thought about my 75-year-old mother hanging onto the outside of the car. You got seasick watching *Sea Hunt* on TV; the thought of you hanging onto the outside of a cable car terrified me. That's why I carefully guided you to an inside seat for your first journey over Nob Hill and down to Fisherman's Wharf. But when I asked you how you liked the ride, you replied with a smile as wide as the Golden Gate, eyes gleaming like the sun bouncing off it, "It was great! But next time," you paused as if surprising yourself by what you were about to ask, "can we ride on the outside?"

Mom and me riding the cable cars in San Francisco

I have to say I was thunderstruck. But for the rest of our visit there, that's what we did. To this day, I can't see a cable car on TV without seeing you hanging on with one hand, waving with the other, and laughing all the way down to the wharf.

I think my sense of humor comes from you. I used to think it came from Dad, but now I realize that's because I rarely gave you credit for anything. You were the subservient wife, a homemaker with no skills beyond cooking and cleaning. I never thought you were smart. I don't remember what incident happened that caused us to nickname you, "Dummy," but cruelly we did. We even addressed your Mother's Day and birthday cards that way. And in camaraderie, I embraced the moniker, "Little Dummy."

It took me years to fully own my intelligence. Maybe that was because Jarrett (my brother) had so much more book-smarts than I, but I now think this family "joke" played a part. I wonder what it did to you—a woman who possessed the ego and self-confidence of a snail.

You were obsessed with TV. And, as far as I could tell, had no interests, desires, or talents to occupy your time, so TV was all there was for you. When your work was done—the house clean, dinner put away, and the dishwasher running—you sat down in front of the TV. On most nights, you stayed there until a disembodied male voice woke you from your dozing by announcing the station you were watching was signing off for the night. The National Anthem lulled you to sleep too many nights to count.

For years, you didn't read because you couldn't see the words on the page. I finally figured out you were too vain to get glasses. Jarrett and Dad consumed science fiction like they were planning to be astronauts. When Dad returned home from his work travels, conversations about what they were reading, interspersed with animated discussions of football games and strategy, hummed alongside the ever-present television soundscape. When you eventually overcame your vanity and got reading glasses, the world changed for you, but I was already gone by then, so I never knew in what ways.

I don't know if I respected you growing up. I respected you as my mother. That's what good kids were expected to do back then. I never really knew you, though. I knew what you expected of me. To be ladylike. To be polite. To not tattle. But the details of your life I gathered like the crumbs you swept up from the kitchen floor after hosting a dinner party for Dad's co-workers.

As a grown woman now, some would say an old woman, I've come to believe that people have a right to their secrets. I would be a hypocrite if I believed differently. I've spent much of my life in the closet. Until I was in my forties, I selectively chose to reveal that I was a lesbian to those whom I wanted to know. You knew it, of course, but only after Sister Barbara Ann revealed it to you, and then later, after failing to live straight, I told you myself that it wasn't going away. You didn't receive the news well. You believed my sexual orientation was punishment from God for your sins. You never told me what your sins were.

I always knew you had secrets. There was so much you wouldn't talk about. "If you only knew," you would say, but you never chose to enlighten me. I didn't know your secrets were about me. I didn't know you lied to me. I know that now, and I will tell you, it hurts. I imagine it's a pain like the one you carried with you when you learned that I was not going to grow out of my love for women.

It's been a few years now since I've learned as much as is knowable about your secrets. In that time, I've come to realize that my pain is not as much from you as it is about you. It's from knowing the freedom of living in the truth—a freedom you never afforded yourself. I wish I could give that to you. I wish I could let you know that I know. I wish we could talk about it, so you could know I forgive you for lying to me about who I am.

I'm not saying I've come to this place easily. I'm not saying I'm not angry about what you did. I'm not saying I'm not hurt that you lied to me. I am saying that I wish you could know the freedom that comes from living in the truth. I wish you still had the chance to forgive yourself. I even wish we could find a way to laugh about it. Something in it all must be funny.

Letter 2

Dear Mom,

Do you remember the question we often got when you introduced Jarrett and me to another grown-up? Before they even started speaking, I knew what was coming. All they had to do was look at us with their sweet smiles. "Where'd you get your red hair?" they'd ask, as if they expected us to say that our fairy godmother had pointed her wand at us and accidentally caught our hair on fire. I answered that question so many times I got to the point that I had to suppress a giggle before I could cough up a response.

Our red hair captivated people. The rarest of all hair colors, red hair holds mystery, imagination, and power that other hair colors just can't match. I'm sure the people who asked us where our red hair came from didn't mean any harm—it was their way of saying how special we were—but it always made me uncomfortable. I never knew what to say, and, in my snarkier teenage moments, replied, "Oh, my mom craved strawberries when she was pregnant with me." They would laugh, and I would be able to move on. You did crave strawberries, right, Mom?

The truth is, I didn't know. What I knew was that you had black hair before it turned a stunning silver, and from what you told us, so did our deceased father, i.e., your first husband, Bob, and your first daughter, Marlee.

Conveniently, Norm, the second man you married when I was five, who then legally adopted Jarrett and me, had red hair, so whenever adults asked me, "Where'd you get your red hair?" I started answering, "From our dad, he has red hair."

Although I knew it was a lie, answering this way made me feel more like we were a normal family, like Norm was our real father who had passed on his curly, red hair to his children. That's what he wanted—to be seen as our real dad—that's what you wanted, too. It's what we all wanted.

It was a harmless little lie. Or so I thought. But it became the first loose thread in the unraveling of your deepest secret.

As I write this, I realize that I don't remember ever seeing Dad (Norm)'s red hair. He was 49 when I was born and had already lost most of his hair. The photos I have of him when he's not wearing a hat and before his hair turned grey are in black and white, so I can only take it on faith that he even had red hair. His younger brother, Bernard, had red hair. I remember his. In fact, he went by the nickname "Red," so I'm pretty sure Dad's curly locks were indeed red.

My hair's no longer red, Mom. I first realized it when a hairdresser responded to a casual comment I made about my hair color. "Oh, you used to be a redhead?" she asked. Her words cut as deeply as if she had taken the scissors and stabbed me in the neck. *How could she think I wasn't a redhead? Of course, I was a redhead. I AM a redhead!*

Being a redhead was part of my identity, much like being Catholic. I still think of myself as a redhead, even though I eventually admitted that my hair color became something other than red. A new hairdresser once called it "champagne." I liked that. At least it was still different. She said people pay a lot of money to get hair my color.

After I lost my hair to chemo, it came back much whiter. Much curler too. Although the curls will probably relax over time, I think the color is here to stay. Being a redhead on the inside, though, is something I'll never lose. I imagine it's like a cherished limb, now amputated, that continues to signal pain.

You never liked things that were different, Mom, things that stood out. I wonder what you thought about our red hair. Did it make you uncomfortable to be around us in public? Was it too showy? Did it expose too much of the secret you wanted so desperately to hide?

I didn't like my hair much as a teenager. It was not only red, but thick and wavy when the style was blonde, long, and straight. Even then, I couldn't be straight! And I certainly never fit in.

If my red hair made you uncomfortable, it was only the first of many things about me that made you squirm. In elementary school, you thought I was too bossy. And remember the day you asked me why I always had my arm around all the other little girls? I didn't know that I did, but I stopped myself after that. And what about all the times you told me I wasn't ladylike enough? I hated wearing dresses, preferred exploring the woods or shooting baskets over playing with dolls or other girly pursuits. I was not the girl you wanted me to be.

By the time I was a teenager, it was my weight that worried you—still skinny by today's standards but heftier than you thought I should be. You were so afraid I would get fat that it became one of the only things we talked about. Until, that is, you found out I was a lesbian. Then we stopped talking about anything important.

That's when you knew you were defeated. I would never become the daughter you dreamed of having, the daughter to replace the one taken from you by polio before I was even born. You had lost, not just the battle, but the war.

Sadly, you believed it was your sins that had done you in. God was punishing you for some unspeakable sin or sins, and that's why I turned out the way I did. If only you could have told me the truth, especially about my red hair. I hope I would have listened and tried to understand. It's what I longed for from you when you learned my truth—that you'd listen and try to understand. I think I could have done that then for you. I know I could now. I've lived too complicated a life to not have developed deep compassion for the choices people make, right or wrong, explicable or inexplicable. I would still love you, Mom, if you had told me the truth.

But there is no "now" available to us anymore because you're gone. All I can do is tell my story and what pieces of yours I've been able to stitch together. There will always be unraveled threads. Without you or Dad showing me where to put the pieces, all I can do is follow the strands that lead me somewhere and let the others go. I don't know if it will ever be enough, but I will always cherish what I learn about the truth, just like I cherish the memory of my red hair.

Letter 3

Dear Mom,

Unlike a lot of my friends who are dealing with parents in their eighties and nineties, both you and Dad are already gone. Can you believe Dad's been dead for over forty-five years? I have to say I have a hard time remembering him. He's like some ghostly figure who appears to me in a dream. I figured out that I only actually lived with him for eleven years. You married him when I was five, and I went away to school when I was sixteen. With all the traveling he did for work, he was probably only home fifty percent or even less of that time. He died when I was twenty-two. I was already long gone from home at that time. I know he loved me, but we didn't really know each other.

Pretty much everyone from your generation has died. Uncle Bernard's wife Opal is still alive—she's in her 90s now, probably nearing 100, but even some of my older cousins, especially on Dad's side, have died or started to occupy nursing homes and assisted living centers. That's because you were forty and forty-two, respectively, when Jarrett and I were born. Dad was seven years older than you. I don't know how you kept up with two toddlers. If I'd had a kid at the age that you had me, they'd be twenty-six now, out of college and trying to start their life in the aftermath of the COVID-19 pandemic.

It's been a mess here, Mom, since the pandemic hit. I suspect it's not unlike 1949, the year Marlee died of polio. I'm glad you didn't have to live through the COVID shutdown. You wouldn't have enjoyed the confinement, the anxiety, and, especially, the vitriol.

It was especially hard for elderly people and kids, and it would have reminded you too much of the polio epidemic. So many deaths since the pandemic started in 2020. And the saddest part? We have a vaccine that too many people still refuse to get. If only there had been a vaccine when Marlee got sick. Although I probably would have never been born, I suspect your life would have been much happier.

My point in all this is that this is not the best time to go on a quest to uncover the truth about a long-buried family secret. Everyone who knows anything is already gone, and, while you all were living, I never asked you or anyone else who might have known answers to the questions that haunt me now.

Early on in my life, I developed an aversion to asking questions. I either accepted things at face value or kept my questions to myself. Maybe it was because of all those people asking about my red hair. I suspect, though, it was something much more deeply-seeded than that—something in our family's culture that discouraged questions. You never liked to pry. I assume that's because you didn't want anyone to pry back.

It's ironic that my faith community now, Unitarian Universalism, is all about asking questions. One of our most revered hymns, We Laugh, We Cry, by Shelley Jackson Denham, ends with the words "even to question, truly is an answer." That was not how you raised me, though. Our Roman Catholic faith discouraged questions, and I worked hard at being a good Catholic kid. Some of my friends now joke that they were thrown out of Catechism class because they asked too many questions. I was never thrown out of class. I bought it all hook, line, and sinker.

Perhaps that's why, for much of my life, I accepted your perfectly acceptable story about who our father was. I now know that story was a lie.

I wince every time I say that. It's hard for me to think of you as a liar. It's especially hard to think that you and Dad (Norm) conspired to lie to us. I suspect that Dad crafted the story and convinced you to go along with it. Yet, for some reason, I mostly blame you for it. You're the one who told us the story—you're the one who perpetuated the lie. Dad rarely talked about it. He was just happy to be our dad.

I know now, Mom, why you were so anxious all the time, why you worried so much, why you never felt at home in your own skin. You were terrified that your secret would be exposed.

Did Aunt Babe know? She had to have. Is that why you felt an obligation to take care of her even though you didn't really like her? What about Billy, the brother you couldn't stand? What did he know? Were they critical of the choices you made, and is that why there was so much tension between you? You once told me that Babe never helped you out after Bob died. Was that why? Was it because she knew the truth and didn't approve of what you had done?

I'll never know the answers to many of these questions, but that doesn't stop me from aching to understand, Mom, from working to piece together the truth from a tattered cloth you wore thin by trying to rub your sins away.

Letter 4

Dear Mom,

In my work in the chemical dependency field in the 1980s (Do you remember when you came to visit me at the treatment center I ran, Mom, and how impressed you were with the work I did?), we taught our patients about the Johari Window, a tool developed by Joseph Luft and Harrington Ingram[1] to help people understand themselves and how they interact with others. It consists of a four-square grid in which you can examine your public and private self and your conscious and unconscious self.

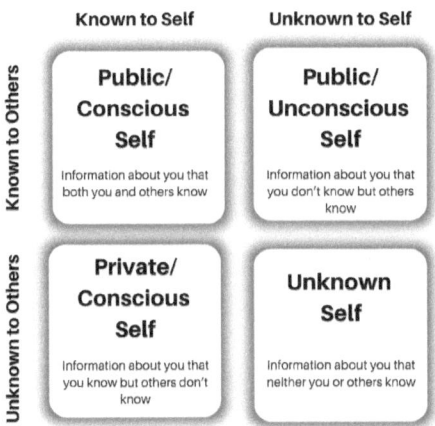

The Johari Window

I've found it helpful in understanding myself and my life story and in thinking about what I want to change about myself. Here's what each quadrant means.

Public/Conscious (Open) Self

In the top left quadrant of the Johari Window is the Public/Conscious Self, the part of you that is known to you and to others around you. This is the visible you that people who know you would recognize when they hear you describe yourself. For example, I'm a white woman in her late sixties who was born in Michigan, grew up in Arkansas, and then returned to Michigan for school and a substantial part of my life.

Although I've also lived in Colorado, Massachusetts, Illinois, and North Carolina, I now live in Richmond, Virginia, with my wife, Wendy (yes, I got married, Mom, in 2010, but more about that at a later date). I have an active spiritual life as part of my Unitarian Universalist faith. I'm a social justice/civil rights activist, writer, and tech lover.

I have a wide range of skills that friends and employers have come to rely on. I'm calm in crisis situations, practical in everyday life, and dependable in my commitments. Although I've moved around a lot, both geographically and relationally, I work hard to keep people—friends, and even some of my exes—in my life.

I've always struggled with my weight—since the time between 7th and 8th grade when I came home from a month at Aunt Babe's, and you decried that I had gained twenty pounds. "Must have been all those hamburgers and all that pie!" you declared. For the first time in my life, and from that moment on, I felt your disgust about who I was.

These are things that most people who get to know me can easily learn about me. They are things I would have told you, or you would have learned about me when you visited, even though I know you didn't like "cause" people.

Public/Unconscious (Blind) Self

The top right square in the Johari Window is the Blind (or Public/Unconscious) Self. It's the part of you that is known to others and not to you. It might be a personality trait that annoys people, such as you laugh too loudly at a party, or a trait that people admire, like you always go the extra mile to help someone out. In either case, you're not conscious of the behavior; it's just who you are.

A personal development goal could be to become aware of how others see you, learn what they know about you that you don't, and uncover experiences that impacted you that you don't remember. As a child, I always had the feeling that other people, especially you and Dad, for starters, knew things about me that I didn't know. As an adult, I've discovered what some of those things were, and that's why I feel a need to tell this story.

Private/Conscious (Hidden) Self

The bottom left square in the Johari Window is the Hidden (or Private/Conscious) Self—that part of you that you and only you know—your innermost thoughts and feelings, escapades that you never told anyone about, secrets you keep. Moving what's inside me to my public self has always been challenging to me. I don't show my feelings easily. Some people have even said they experience me as aloof and difficult to get to know. I'm sure I get those traits from you. It's better not to expose yourself to others for fear they might judge you.

I have to trust before I share much about me. This was especially true before I came out as a lesbian. Although I'm much more open today than I ever was as a younger person (as evidenced by this memoir), sharing myself with others is an ongoing part of my spiritual journey. This is where you guarded the family secret(s), Mom, praying no one would ever find out.

Private/Unconscious (Unknown) Self

Which leads me to the last window square in the bottom right corner, the Unknown Self. This is the part that is not known to you or anyone else: your hidden motivations and desires, things you don't understand about why you do what you do. With honest self-examination, reflection, and openness, some of what's hidden here can become known, at least to your private self.

As I've grown older, this has become an even more critical part of my journey, to better understand my actions, motivations, and responses to life's events. To do that, I must be willing to learn things I don't want to know, to accept my own shortcomings, to admit to myself that, even in my sixties, I might have some things to learn about myself.

The greatest struggle of my life has been to lift the shade on the Johari Window, to let in the light, especially to understand, accept, and maybe even forgive the lies on which my life was built—those told to me and those I told to others.

Your secret didn't fully unravel until I turned fifty years old, four years after you, at the age of eighty-eight, slipped away in your sleep at Jarrett's house. Maybe it's good you weren't alive when I learned the truth. I don't know if I ever could have confronted you with it, and I don't know how we could have had a relationship with this unspoken thing between us.

You taught me to never make waves. As you well know, I've not always heeded that advice. I've made plenty of waves in my life, especially when it comes to challenging injustice and violence I see around me, but would I have ever been able to talk with you about this? I honestly don't know. I guess that's why I'm talking to you now, why I'm exposing your secrets to the world in this way.

Don't get me wrong, I've certainly questioned myself about whether it's my story to tell. Do I have the right to tell your secrets, the choices you made, the lies you told? Is that fair to you to tarnish your memory? These are the questions of every responsible memoirist, and the answers are never easy.

In this case, I've come down on the side of yes. I was indelibly impacted by the choices you made. I've had to heal the pain you caused me, and I've had to find a way to understand how it has affected me. This is my story to tell. It's my hope that it will benefit others who are trying to heal from similar deceptions.

If you were still alive, I would encourage you to tell it with me. It's hard to imagine you could ever do that—you carried too much shame for that—but I truly believe it would result in genuine healing for both of us. I hope you could have seen that too.

I've said all I want to say to you now in these letters, Mom. It's time to start telling the story I've uncovered. I hope your spirit will guide me if I get something wrong. I'll do the best I can, be as honest as I can be, and lift as much of the shade on the Johari window as possible. I also hope your spirit will understand how important it is for the truth to be known.

I love you, Mom.

Your daughter,
Annette

1. Luft, J.; Ingham, H. (1955). "The Johari window, a graphic model of interpersonal awareness". *Proceedings of the Western Training Laboratory in Group Development.* Los Angeles: University of California, Los Angeles.

Part One

CHAPTER ONE

You Can Call Him Dad

No other trip my mom had taken in her life could compare to the train ride to Denver. This was a trip into the unknown from which she could never return. It happened in the summer of 1960, just after I turned five, when my mom, my older brother, Jarrett, and I boarded a train in Ann Arbor, Michigan, bound for Denver, Colorado. Mom was a petite woman, only 5'2" with heels. Convinced that, at her height, she couldn't afford an extra pound, she worked hard to maintain her weight. She always wore make-up—mascara, rouge, lipstick—but it rarely looked overdone. A prominent widow's peak foretold her life to anyone who was listening. She had wavy, black hair with silver streaks—fitting for her forty-seven years—but unusual for a mother with two children under seven. Her hair was the kind of silver-gray that sophisticated women spent hours seeking—and paying for—at the beauty parlor. But to Mom, it just meant she stood out from her friends—all of them ten or even twenty years younger than she—and standing out was the last thing she ever wanted. Mom was happiest when she was in the background, helping others shine, especially when it was her kids.

She was probably well-dressed for the journey, in a skirt, jacket, and pressed white blouse—as she would dress for church—because that is what you did when you traveled. She would have carried a purse, not too big, just enough for her leather clutch wallet with the gold metal clasp at the top, a white lace handkerchief, a plastic comb, a pink compact with mirror, a tube of red lipstick, a roll of Lifesavers, and of course, our tickets.

Before this trip, I don't think Mom had ever traveled very far from Detroit, where she was born and raised. Over the years, she mentioned visiting relatives in Toledo, of an occasional trip to Ontario, a trip to Wisconsin for her first honeymoon—I still have the large wooden plaque framing a copper relief of the Madonna that she bought there. She also told me of how her mother sent her as a young teen to work as a housekeeper for a couple in Port Huron, a small city in Michigan's Thumb region. That trip ended badly.

"I begged my mother to let me come home," she told me one day when I mentioned a friend who lived in Port Huron. "The man chased me around the kitchen table, trying to get at me."

"Did she let you come home?" I asked, avoiding the threatening question—the one I wanted to ask—"Did he catch you?"

"She did," she replied, "but she never forgave me for it." I was not sure if she meant for coming home, for getting chased, or for getting caught. And I didn't ask.

I always wondered, though. Mom shied away from touch, turned her face to the side when even her kids moved in to give her a goodnight kiss. As I grew into my teen years, I grew to hate that ritual. It felt like rejection every time I tried to kiss her, and all I got was the side of her face.

Mom was the consummate worrier. When Mom worried, she worried about everything. She worried about being late for church on Sunday. She worried about her Super Bowl party guests being upset if their favorite team lost. She worried about how we'd get to school if even a long-shot weather pattern headed our way.

When she worried, she got anxious, she wouldn't sleep, and she fussed over everything and everyone. She fussed because she wanted people she cared about to be happy, for things to go well, for nothing bad to happen. "For nothing bad to happen," isn't that the mantra of so many who have had bad things happen to them, who live in fear of the bad things? That was my mother—always anticipating the worst—though it would be years before I understood why.

So, I imagine she worried long and hard about this trip. But that didn't stop her. Even though she was a worrier, she had a determination about her that drove her to do what she set out to do. For the past five years, she'd been a single parent of toddlers. Her first husband, and the man she told us, and we believed, was our father, Bob, died when she was four months pregnant with me. He left her with no pension and very little, if any, in savings. I'm not sure how she covered expenses. The only income I know she had was a Social Security survivor benefit for widows with two dependent children—about $175 a month—which even then, didn't go far.

So that's why, she told me when I was older, that she packed up our house in Plymouth, one of Detroit's white picket-fence suburbs, and moved to Denver to start a new life with a man who would take care of us.

"We're going to Denver to see Uncle Norm," Mom told us when she announced the trip to us.

I was excited about seeing Uncle Norm. He had moved from Plymouth a couple months before to work as a salesman for Daisy Air Rifles (aka BB guns). He made me laugh and gave me lots of hugs. And I knew what Daisy was because Uncle Norm had already given me a Daisy for Christmas that year, a cap gun and holster that I loved.

Uncle Norm and Aunt Betty were our godparents, not our real aunt and uncle, but I don't remember ever calling them anything else. In Plymouth, where I was born, they were around for every holiday, for trips to the beach, and just about everything else. We saw them more than we saw our real Aunt Babe and Uncle Paul, who lived on a farm just a few miles away. We regularly visited Uncle Norm and Aunt Betty at their restaurant, the Marquis Toll House. I'd help Aunt Betty fill the napkin holders and salt and pepper shakers, and Jarrett would help Jimmy, the cook, bring supplies up from the storeroom in the basement, dipping into one of the no. 10 size cans for a spoonful of coconut while he was there. I'm not sure how much help a couple of toddlers were, but Uncle Norm, Aunt Betty, and the rest of the staff humored us and made us feel at home.

I loved going to the restaurant, especially when Uncle Norm sliced me off a piece of Marquis Chocolate Cake, the house spe-cialty three-layer chocolate cake with chocolate frosting. Jarrett and I would sit at the counter with the restaurant regulars, old men who came every day. They would challenge us to milk-drinking contests and to see how far we could blow drinking-straw wrappers across the room. Eating the cake was my favorite part, though. I can still taste the rich, moist cake as I licked the sweet chocolate frosting off with my tongue and let it dissolve against the roof of my mouth. It became the cake of birthdays and other special events throughout my childhood.

The train left Michigan Central Station in Detroit and headed west along what is now the I-94 Corridor, the first border-to-border toll-free interstate highway in America. In 1960, when we traveled on the Wolverine train, only parts of the interstate were open, so the train route between Detroit and Chicago, which passed through Ann Arbor to pick up a mother and her two small children, was a popular one. From Ann Arbor, the train traveled through Jackson, home of Jackson State Prison, and Albion, an industrial city filled with iron forge factories and parts suppliers for the auto industry, both towns where I would eventually work after college. The train would roll on through Kalamazoo and Dowagiac, the home of Heddon Fishing Lures, a company that would come to be owned by Daisy, and part of the product line Uncle Norm would peddle in sporting goods stores throughout the West. The train would then swing around the base of Lake Michigan and into Chicago's Union Station.

We would have had to change trains in Chicago. I'm sure that meant my mother fretted until the California Zephyr (CZ) bound for Denver pulled out of the station with us aboard. Early in the

CZ's history, the railroad segregated women and children in the first car, but by the time we rode, this was no longer the case—we could have chosen our own seats anywhere on the train. Because the CZ traveled all the way to San Francisco, across the Rocky and Sierra Mountain ranges and through Feather River Canyon in northern California, it boasted a second level of seating high above the rails in its Vista Dome chair cars. To assure passengers enjoyed the most scenic views in daylight, it left Chicago, rumbled through Chicago's warehouse district, and into the small towns and farmland of Northern Illinois, so that by the time it passed into endless flatlands of the Great Plains, it was dark. That meant we probably arrived in Denver, at the east end of the Rockies, in the early morning hours.

I can imagine Mom's anxiety rising again as barren grasslands replaced the lush landscape of her known world. At the time, I wasn't cognizant of Mom's emotional state, but in looking back at it, I'm certain worry would have consumed her—worry for us, worry for herself, even worry for the other passengers on the train.

All I remember is that somewhere close to Denver, Mom freshened us up and prepared us to disembark. After we were looking smart, she stood us, my brother and I, next to each other, put one hand on each of our shoulders, my right, and Jarrett's left, and said something like, "Kids, I want you to listen to me. When we see Uncle Norm at the station, you can call him Dad."

Because we were standing up at the time, I suspect we might have already pulled into Denver's Union Station. I don't remember if the morning sun had started to peek over the horizon we had left behind. I don't remember if I felt the morning chill against my five-year-old arms. I also don't remember if the whistle was blowing as the train rumbled into a more populated area, but I'm pretty sure it was, because whenever I hear a train whistle today, I think of that moment, of Mom's words, "You can call him Dad."

I can still transport myself back into my tiny body with a head full of curly red hair. I can still feel Mom's hands on me while she fussed with my clothes. I can feel my eyes getting big and something fluttering fast in my chest as I heard her say, "Dad." I was too young to understand much of what was going on, but I liked it when people were happy, and Mom sounded happy, and Jarrett seemed happy, and I imagined Uncle Norm—I mean, Dad,—would be happy to see us, so that was enough for me.

As dawn broke in the Denver sky, we stepped off the train and greeted our new dad. I don't know if we actually said, "Hi, Dad." I do remember that he leaned down to Jarrett and me, kissed each of us, and then grabbed us close to his rotund body with one hand, as he reached out to grasp our mother's hand with the other. No doubt two pipes loaded with tobacco protruded from his belt and a pair of glasses sat precariously atop his bald head. When I felt his arms around us, it was like the engine had just locked on to complete the train. You can call him Dad.

"I'm so glad you're here. How was the trip? Did you have fun on the train?" I can imagine him peppering Jarrett and me with questions about our experiences as he continued to hold Mom's hand. I noticed that, and it made me smile. Mom seemed stiff, un-comfortable, as she always did with outward displays of affection, but Dad made up for it with his warmth and enthusiasm about having his new family together. I was glad he seemed so happy.

When Mom and Dad finally got the first hug of their new life together, I wormed myself in between them to make sure they knew it included me. I don't think I really feared it wouldn't. In fact, I don't think it took me any time to adjust to the idea of having a dad. I don't think I questioned how it happened that Uncle Norm became our dad or whatever ever became of Aunt Betty. He had been so much a part of our lives before, and now we got to have more of him. That was all I knew to care about.

CHAPTER TWO

Making It Official

E xcept for serving in the Navy during World War II, and a few out of state jobs he took to survive the Great Depression, Norman William Marquis (who I refer to interchangeably in this chapter as "Norm" and "Dad") lived his whole life in Michigan. His Roman Catholic parents Anne Marie Cheff and William Patrick Marquis emigrated to Detroit's nearest suburb, River Rouge, Michigan, from Ontario, Canada before their oldest son, Norman, was born in 1907.

He always said the Irish side of him, including his red hair, came from his father with the French last name. I never understood what he meant by that until I heard from my cousins that there were rumors that Dad's father was adopted. Pipi died in 1933, long before we ever could have known him. The only time I remember Dad mentioning him was to tell us that he was born on the Fourth of July. He failed to mention that his father was adopted—that he didn't know any of his Irish relatives. Perhaps that's where Dad first learned to keep family secrets.

Regardless of where it came from, Dad loved his Irish side, from the blandness of a corned beef and cabbage boiled dinner to the excitement of a Fighting Irish football game. Every car we ever owned, except for one blue Chevy Impala station wagon, was green. A photo from the 1950s shows he had a green car even then.

After high school, Norman spent a short time in seminary to be a Catholic priest. He never said why he left. He spent the years before the war working for the Detroit and Cleveland Navigation Company and the McCarthy Steamship Company, where he was the supervisor of auto shipping. I never heard him mention his work there, like those years were packed up into a can of Spam, a food he thought more vile than death by starvation. I learned about his steamship days when I discovered a yellowed half sheet of paper with a bio of him typed in red ink and all caps, notes you might give someone to introduce you at a speaking event.

In 1939, when Dad was thirty-two, he moved to Plymouth, Michigan, and married a woman named Betty. Norm was her fourth husband. Family lore was that Betty's daughter from a previous marriage had substance abuse problems, and so Norm and Betty raised her son Lee and to some extent, her older daughter Lorraine. They had no children of their own, at least that I'm aware of.

Three years after he married, Dad joined the Navy's Construction Battalions known as the SeaBees, and spent four years shuffling between Rhode Island, Panama Canal, and Pearl Harbor, until finally landing on Enewetak Atoll in the South Pacific, where he served as a mailman. Like many men who served in World War

II, he was proud of his service and spoke of it frequently. He often joked that a bullet had caused the indentation and adjacent incision in his stomach but, in reality, he never saw combat. I believe that killing someone would have troubled him deeply, so I'm glad he never had to.

Upon his discharge as a 1st Class Petty Officer, Norm opened a restaurant in Plymouth with Betty. Located right on Main Street, the Marquis Toll House became a community landmark and a gathering place for movers and shakers in this small town that more closely resembled a New England village than a southeastern Michigan city. Many of his customers worked for Daisy Manufacturing Company, home of the Daisy BB gun, which was located just a block away.

In addition to being active in Our Lady of Good Counsel Catholic Church, Dad served as president of the local chapter of the American Cancer Society, the Lions Club, the Plymouth Community Fund, and on the St. Mary's Catholic Hospital board of directors in Livonia, a city where I would later live with my life-partner. In addition to these community involvements, he founded and served as chair of the Republican Club and was elected Wayne County supervisor.

I don't know exactly when and how he and Mom met. A newspaper clipping shows Mom's husband, Bob, serving as treasurer of the Republican Club of Plymouth, when Norm served as chair. Is that how they met or was it through the church? At the restaurant? At some other community event? I doubt I'll ever know.

What I do know is that when Jarrett was born in 1953, Uncle Norm and Aunt Betty stood beside Mom and Bob at his baptism.

Being Jarrett's godfather, and later mine, was the first formal role Uncle Norm played in our lives.

Mom was four months pregnant with me when Bob died. I don't know a lot about that time. What I know is from brief snippets that escaped Mom's closely guarded vault of secrets. What's truth and what's fiction will never be known for certain. Mom was left alone with a two-year boy and another child on the way. I know very little about how she coped. From 8mm family movies and photographs, I have evidence that our godparents were frequent visitors to our home; we went to community celebrations, like 4th of July parades, together, and, of course, spent time at the restaurant. I don't know if they helped Mom financially, at least in any direct way, but I know they offered support and care to this grieving widow.

This kind of community visibility that Norm enjoyed must have made it difficult for him and my mom as their relationship grew. Although she was now a widow, he was still a married man. I imagine that's why he closed the restaurant he loved and took a job with Daisy—a sales job based in Denver—one that would allow him to quietly divorce his wife and move out of the community he had given so much to and had given so much to him and welcome a new family into his life.

Jarrett and I loved our new dad. He adored us and especially loved to make us laugh. He was like a Saturday matinee I'd sneak in to watch repeatedly without ever paying admission. Storytelling came naturally to him, and it didn't take much prompting to get him to launch into one. One of his favorites went something like this.

"You think it's hot here?" Dad would quip when one of us complained about the heat on a summer's day. "When I was on Enewetak, it was so hot that when I'd deliver mail, the glue would melt on the envelopes, and the letters would fall out in my bag. I'd have to read each one to figure out who to deliver them to." A mischievous grin would creep over his face, which he'd cover up by taking a long drag on his pipe.

"In fact, it was so hot," he'd continue, "we would take our shirts off and pin our medals to our bare chests."

"Oooooh, Dad, that's gross!" I'd exclaim.

"Yeah, we'd pinch a little of our skin like this," he'd say as he demonstrated with the skin on his ample chest. Dad was an All-State lineman on his high school football team thirty years before, and like many ex-football players, his muscle had dissolved into fat. Dad's rotund torso made it hard to imagine him in a sailor's uniform.

"You have to be careful not to pinch too much," he'd explain, "or it'll hurt. But if you stick the pin through the outer skin, you barely feel it. See like this." He'd then pretend he was sticking a pin through his skin. "Some guys would have a whole chest full of them. It sure beats wearing a shirt."

"Dad, stop it!" I'd say. "I'm going to get sick!"

He'd just laugh. His belly would shake, and he'd reach out to hug me. He'd wrap his arms around me, and I could smell the fresh Edgeworth tobacco in the pipes he kept loaded at his waist like handguns he might pull out if anyone came to harm us.

I didn't learn until much later that Uncle Norm, now Dad, had divorced Aunt Betty to marry Mom. At the time we arrived in Denver, I was too young to understand such things, so I didn't know that or its implications. According to their marriage license, which I found after they had both died, Mom and Dad were married in a civil ceremony in Colorado Springs, on a Monday afternoon in December 1961, a year and a half after we moved in with him. I suspect now that they had to wait to get married until his divorce from Betty was final. Until I saw the marriage license, though, I never imagined that my parents lived together (in sin) only pretending they were married.

Jarrett and I would have been in school on their wedding day. I was in first grade, and he was in third. We knew nothing about the wedding.

I can imagine Mom walking us to school and then hurrying home to change into a nice pastel or beige dress, something she would wear to church on Sunday. She probably put on long white gloves and covered her hair with a lace chapel veil she used to wear to church sometimes when she and I still had to cover our hair for Mass. Dad would have worn a suit and tie, probably green.

I don't know why they didn't get married in Denver. Instead, they drove ninety minutes away to Colorado Springs. Perhaps it was all part of the subterfuge.

Mom would have been nervous about getting there and back by the time we got out of school. Because it was a civil ceremony, it would have been fast, a few words, a quick kiss, sign the papers, and they were out of there. Dad would have insisted they go out to a nice lunch, but Mom would have been too anxious about getting home to eat much. I don't know what they would have talked about on the drive—I never knew them to have in-depth conversations about much of anything, but I'd like to imagine that this once they might have found something important to say to each other.

Although Mom and Dad kept their wedding a secret, they didn't hide our adoptions. Sometime after we stepped off the train, probably soon after the wedding, Dad filed papers to legally adopt Jarrett and me. Mom and Dad told us they were doing it so we would legally be Dad's kids. The final decree of adoption is dated July 17, 1962, about the time we moved from Denver to Daisy's home office in Rogers, Arkansas, for Dad's new job as Daisy's retail sales manager. The papers said, "the court doth find that the petitioner, Norman W. Marquis, has good moral character, ability to support and educate said child, and a suitable home.

It goes on to say, "The said, Robert Leo Smith, the natural father of said child, is deceased; that the said Helen M. Marquis, the natural mother of said child, has given her written, notarized, consent to said adoption without however, relinquishing any of her rights to the said child."

On the adoption decree, my middle name, Suzanne, is misspelled as Suzan. The full name of the child, Annette Suzan Smith, has the appearance of a mysterious stranger, someone I used to know but about whom I can only recall foggy details. Mom and Dad were both part French and, when the adoption was final, I became all French, at least in name—Annette Suzanne Marquis—a French name, perfectly balanced with seven letters in each. My new identity felt strong and stable. Finally, we were a real family, and I was a part of it. I knew who I was and where I belonged.

It wasn't until I was in college that I thanked Mom for marrying Dad to save me from the initials she bestowed on me at my birth —A.S.S. (Annette Suzanne Smith).

"Oh, my achin' back!", she said, mortified by the realization, "I would never have done that on purpose!" She confessed that she wasn't thinking all that clearly back then, which I could understand given that her husband had just died, and she had a toddler and new baby to care for.

As an irreverent teenager, I thought my original initials were hysterical and wished I still had them. I kidded her about it endlessly. But it made me wonder if subconsciously she knew my name wouldn't last long enough for it to become a target of ridicule.

Me, Dad, and Jarrett in Denver a year before our adoptions

In the weeks and months that followed our arrival in Denver, Dad told us repeatedly how much he loved being our father. "I love you kids so much. I hope you know that," he'd say and then look at us like he was waiting for us to say something back.

"Sure, Dad," Jarrett would say. He was older so I let him do the talking, but I would crawl up onto Dad's lap and put my arms around his neck. The sweet but burnt scent of pipe tobacco distinguished his from any other lap. He would take the pipe out of his mouth, and with the bowl in his palm and the stem protruding from the fingers of his hand, he would reach for Jarrett. Jarrett would crawl up on his other knee and directly into one of Dad's humongous hugs. I felt so safe there with his arms around us like that, even when the pipes on his belt would poke into my side. I was glad he was now our dad.

So, that's why, from that point on, whenever adults asked me, "Where'd you get your red hair?" I answered automatically, without a second thought, "From our dad, he has red hair."

CHAPTER THREE

Learning to Lie

Sitting on the ground by the chain-link fence between our Denver yards, I watched the little dark-haired girl in the yard next door with curiosity. Perhaps two or three years older than me, she moved with a grace I didn't have, although I'm not sure I would have known to label it that way at five. What I knew then is that I liked watching her pirouette around her small, shaded yard. She turned somersaults and cartwheels from one side of the yard to the other. When she finally plunked herself down by the fence opposite me, sweat poured off her face and her shiny black hair took its time settling back onto her shoulders.

"Hi," she said.

"Hi," I said back.

I don't know what the content of our conversation was after that. I imagine she told me her name—Margo—and I told her mine. I might have told her that we just moved here from Michigan. She might have told me that she'd lived there all her life. The only thing I remember her saying as clearly as if she sat across the room from me at this moment, are these words:

"I hope you're not Catholic. We hate Catholics."

Even now, I can feel my little red-haired self freeze like a cartwheel suspended in mid-air. The birds stopped singing. The color drained from the trees. Everyone in my life up to this point, at least as far as I knew, was Catholic. Well, except Aunt Babe and Uncle Paul. They were farmers, and God excused them from going to church on Sunday because they had chores to do. They were Catholics in their hearts, or so I thought. I was sure of that. In fact, at that time, I didn't know you could be anything but Catholic.

I was too young to know the Catholic teachings about standing up for one's faith, about how martyrs like St. Stephen were put to death for refusing to disavow their beliefs and that that's what made them martyrs in the first place. Years later, when I was ten or eleven and old enough to know about such things, I sat in my catechism class and dreamed of being a martyr for Jesus, I'm not sure I reflected on this moment as evidence that I had what it takes.

What I knew was that in the same way I had red hair, I was Catholic, and I couldn't lie about it. "We are," I said.

I don't know what Margo said next. I don't know what else I said. I just know that, as a young adult, the first time I sat in an anti-racism training session and was asked to tell the person next to me about my first memory of being different, I remembered this moment. I remembered Margo's somersaults and cartwheels. I remembered her shiny black hair. I remembered the chain link fence between us and the hard ground underneath my tiny body. I remembered feeling empty inside like she had reached in and grabbed my guts and pulled them through the wire fence. It was the first time that someone had said they hated me for who I was. I wish I could say it was the last.

Somehow, in the way little kids do, we got through this difficult encounter. I don't know if it was immediate, or if it took some time. What I know is that Margo became my first best friend.

For the two short years we lived in Denver, I attended first grade at St. James Catholic School, went to Mass every school day, every Sunday, and every Holy Day of Obligation, and began to learn about martyrs, saints, and what it meant to be a Catholic. Margo attended her public school and her Protestant church. But in our free time, we were inseparable. We played school on our front porches. She tried to teach me to turn cartwheels. She'd sneak over at night so we could talk through my bedroom window. She came to my sixth birthday party and pinned the tail on the donkey. Even her parents were friendly to my parents, as good neighbors were in those days, despite their feelings about our faith.

My parents worked hard to make my brother and me good Catholic kids. They told us to be nice to people no matter who they are, be polite to grown-ups, always tell the truth. At the same time, they told us not to tell anyone, even my best friend Margo, that Dad had been married before. Some stuff, they said, was just for the family to know.

That was the beginning of my lessons in how to keep secrets.

Without question, I was a happy child in the years we lived in Denver. My parents loved me. I had a good mix of school and play. My best friend lived right next door. And I loved going on summer trips with Dad to explore the Rocky Mountains and surrounding countryside. Dad's sales territory included Colorado, Wyoming, Montana, and the Dakotas, and what better way to sell Daisy guns to Western Auto dealers and local hardware stores in small western towns than to be accompanied by a live six-year-old model.

I loved being a cowboy and felt immensely more myself wearing my vest, hat, and holster than I ever did in a dress holding a doll. If I wasn't dressed as a cowboy, I often chose to go without a shirt. I don't know how old I was when my mother told me that I couldn't do that anymore, but I'm sure she did. It's striking to me now that someone, probably my father, felt perfectly OK about taking a photo of his little shirtless girl.

It was around this time that I first remember lying to avoid trouble. My first-grade classroom was in a small brick building across the street from the main school and church buildings. At lunchtime, we would put on our coats, line up alphabetically in single file at the front of the classroom, and then follow Sister Mary Robert across the street, up the stairs, down the long hallway, and into the cafeteria. We would sit at long wooden tables, like never-ending picnic tables with benches built in, and wait for cafeteria volunteers, like my mother, to bring us our trays. I imagine we were too young to be counted on to successfully carry our own trays without dropping them, so we waited as patiently as first graders could for our food to be delivered to us.

On the day in question, my tray arrived and was placed in front of me. I don't know if my mom put it there or if one of the other mothers did. What I remember is seeing two yeast rolls balanced precariously on the edge of my brightly colored plate— white, puffy rolls, lightly browned at the top and edges, smelling of yeast and dough, with a little hint of sweet. What I remember is that I gagged.

I gagged a lot at that age. At practically every meal something made me gag. I suspect I might have had undiagnosed food allergies, perhaps to the first wave of processed foods that found their way to our plates in the late fifties and early sixties. But back then, if it was on your plate, you ate it. You did not waste food. Whether it was for the starving children in Africa or the saintly virtue of being thankful for what you were given, cleaning our plates was right up there with honoring our fathers and mothers. I sometimes wondered why it wasn't one of The Ten Commandments, but then, I wasn't sure which one it could replace because The Eleven Commandments just didn't sound right.

Notwithstanding, the thought of putting those rolls into my mouth was too much for me. At a moment when my mother wasn't looking, when Sister Mary Robert engaged in conversation with one of the mothers or attended to another of my classmates, I did the unconscionable. I slipped the rolls off my plate and onto the floor. Nestled between rows of little girls' patent leather shoes and boys' loafers, there they rested. If I leaned back and tilted my head just so, I could see them there on the buffed linoleum cafeteria floor.

My heart raced a little when I realized what I'd done—the sin I was sure I'd committed. Even knowing that, though, was better than putting those disgusting rolls in my mouth. According to my daily catechism class, I wouldn't reach the age of reason for another whole year, until I was seven. At that time, I would have to go to confession and tell the priest the bad things I did, but I figured that until then I was safe. What I hadn't considered was the wrath of Sister Mary Robert.

The rest of lunch proceeded without incident, and by the time we put our coats back on, lined up, and headed back to our isolated classroom across the street, I was sure I'd gotten away with it.

It wasn't until the end of the day, just before class was about to be dismissed that Sister Mary Robert addressed us.

She stood at the front of the class with her hands clasped underneath her scapula, the long piece of cloth that hung in front of her habit, and declared, "Someone in this class wasted food today. Someone threw their delicious hot rolls onto the floor of the cafeteria. We are going to stay here until the person who did this comes forward."

I could feel my body stiffen in my seat. I glanced around the room without moving my head—just shifting my eyes from side to side. I waited.

"Well?" Sister Mary Robert asked, "Is anyone going to admit that they did this?" She looked at each of us as if she could read the list of sins engraved on our souls. I forced myself to loosen up, to look normal, to not let her read my list.

I waited some more.

The bell rang, and still no one moved. After what seemed like years, a few mothers came to the classroom door to see why their child hadn't yet been released. My brother and I walked the few blocks to our house every day, so my mother must have waited there, wondering why we were late. I don't know what my brother did—if he waited for me or went home. I just remember sitting there, feeling guilty and ashamed for what might have been the first time in my life. But even that wasn't enough for me to admit my wrongdoing.

I don't know how much time passed before she finally released us. What I know is that I never came forward. Somewhere inside of me, I found a place to keep my secret. There was power in keeping a secret, although I doubt that I would have been able to describe it that way then.

What I knew was that, just like the fact that my dad had been married before, I could keep some things to myself. Was that the same as lying? I'm not sure I tried to differentiate between lying and secret-keeping at the ripe old age of six. All I remember is that I liked knowing things that others didn't, especially if keeping them to myself kept me out of trouble.

Eventually, the roll incident was replaced by another first-grade crime. "Someone in this classroom," Sister intoned, "went into a bathroom stall, locked the door, and then crawled underneath it to leave it locked." She scanned the room with her x-ray eyes. Even though I felt like throwing up, I sat there stoically. I wouldn't let her eyes penetrate me.

I don't know why I did it—why I locked the bathroom door. It was just one of those things that my little first-grade self felt called to do—an early act of rebellion. Maybe it seemed like a magic trick. I loved magic shows, especially when the magician made something disappear or reappear. Maybe when I crawled under the stall door, I imagined myself reappearing in a magic trick.

"We are going to sit here," Sister Mary Robert commanded as she slid into the chair behind her desk, "until someone," (pause for effect), "confesses."

Despite my sweaty palms, I again learned that the best strategy was silence. When no one confessed and she finally released us, all she said was, "Jesus knows, children. Jesus knows." I gulped but walked on out the door.

The next time they served us yeast rolls at lunch, I stuffed them into my mouth, praying I wouldn't throw up all over the cafeteria table. Although I knew how to keep a secret, I also knew it came with a risk of discovery I wasn't willing to take for yucky yeast rolls or silly magic tricks. It would be a few more years before I fully mastered the art of secret-keeping—at a time when the stakes were much higher—but I was on my way.

CHAPTER FOUR

Whisperings

"Marlee would be twenty-eight today," Mom murmured. She and I were the only ones home so I figured she was either talking to me or to herself. I didn't look up from my book. I was curled up in Dad's big, comfy chair and didn't want to be disturbed. Instead, I said, "Wow," and kept on reading. I was in the middle of *The Mystery of the Whispering Mummy*, the third book in the "Alfred Hitchcock and The Three Investigators" series. Mom loved Hitchcock movies and, at age 10, I loved these books.

In this story, Hitchcock asks the boys, Jupiter, Pete, and Bob, to visit a professor friend of his who has a mummy who whispers to him in some mysterious language. The boys' job is to figure out what the mummy is saying and why he's saying it. When Mom's mutterings interrupted me, I'd just reached an exciting part where Jupiter disguises himself as the professor and gets the mummy to whisper to him. For a minute, when Mom spoke, I thought it was the mummy whispering.

"Maybe she'd be going for a horseback ride to celebrate her birthday. She loved horses." She kept talking, a little louder this time.

The horses caught my attention. I finally looked up and saw Mom standing at the kitchen counter. She was staring out the picture window, the one that offered views of thunderstorms crossing the ravine and descending on our house. Northwest Arkansas, the place we'd moved to a couple of years earlier from Denver so Dad could work at the Daisy Manufacturing Company headquarters, was known for its thunderstorms. You could see them coming long before they arrived.

Jarrett and I used to run from one side of the house to the other—from one picture window to the other—to track a storm's path. "It's raining in the back of the house! Is it raining in front?"

"Not raining in front yet!" the other would yell back.

We'd soon correct ourselves, as if the storm heard us and wanted to prove us wrong. "Oh, here it comes!"

And when the rain finally engulfed the entire house, the accompanying lightning and thunder could be vicious.

One time, lightning came through the TV and burned the floor where milliseconds before Jarrett had been lying watching a TV show. Fortunately, the electrical energy that preceded the lightning strike prompted him to pop up and run to the back of the house, so he didn't get burned. We only grasped the danger when we replaced the carpet a short time later and discovered the burned floor.

Today felt like a storm was coming.

Mom's hand clutched a sponge, her arm frozen to the counter. I glanced up to see if she was crying, but I didn't see any tears. No surprise there. Mom didn't cry. Any tears she had stayed locked inside her. Still, I could tell she wanted me to listen to her. I begrudgingly put the mystery down and refocused my attention on another mystery, the story of my sister.

I uncoiled my legs and slipped from the chair so I could lean on the bar that separated the kitchen from the family room—and me from Mom. My book would have to wait. "I wish she could have taught me how to ride," I pined. "I woulda liked that."

I never knew my sister, Marlee. She died of polio six years before I was born when she was only eleven, a year older than I was then. She was Mom and Bob's first child, born in Michigan in 1939, in the waning months of the Great Depression. I don't know when I first learned about Marlee. There must have been a time when Mom told me about her for the first time, a time when I discovered I was not Mom's only daughter, when I learned I was her third child, instead of the younger sister of my first-born brother. But I don't remember when that was.

I'd always wondered what it would be like to have a big sister who could have taught me to ride a real horse. My brother didn't want his little sister hanging around anymore. I figured it might be different with a big sister, even one eighteen years older. Since Mom had already interrupted my reading, I decided to take advantage of this rare opportunity to see if I could find out more about my sister.

"What else did Marlee like, Mom?"

Mom looked at me—a weird smile grew on her face, "She was quiet and liked to curl up with a book, just like you're doing. But she loved her friends, too. She and Marcia loved to go horse-back riding and playing at the beach. Each summer, when we'd go to the beach in Ludington, they'd build big sandcastles." Mom gestured as if the sandcastles were right in front of us. I could almost see them. "And the two of them could swing for hours."

I didn't really like swinging, but maybe if I had a big sister, I would have liked it better. As she described the swing hanging from the old apple tree in the back of their house, Mom started to rock on her feet, like she was swinging right there with her. For a moment, I was jealous—I didn't remember Mom ever pushing me on a swing.

Then, as quickly as she started, Mom stopped rocking. She glared at me as if I'd grabbed the rope holding her imaginary swing. I didn't know what to do so I slunk back to Dad's chair and picked up my book. I didn't feel much like reading anymore, though. Instead, I pretended to read to give Mom her privacy while I thought about how, like The Three Investigators, I had a mystery to solve, a mystery Mom kept locked inside her. I had a feeling that if I knew what it was, I would find out more about Mom and more about me and my red hair. I wished The Three Investigators were around to help me unravel it. Better yet, I wished that, like the mummy in my book, my sister would whisper to me in a language I could understand and tell me everything she knew about our mom.

A couple of years later, Mom told me something that helped me understand her reticence to talk about Marlee. We were in Mom and Dad's bedroom looking through old photographs we kept in a big built-in drawer behind the door. The vertical wooden blinds on the windows made an unsettling noise as the air conditioner came on. The blinds were partway open, allowing just a sliver of light into the room, the way secrets work in my family.

"Your dad made me throw away all the pictures I had of Marlee and Bob," she said, as she shuffled through a stack of photos of Jarrett and me when we were little.

"He what?" I asked. I wasn't sure I heard her right.

"He wanted to be your *only* dad so badly. He didn't want any reminders around of ...what it was like before him," she replied, her voice trailed off at the end of the sentence, and I had to strain to listen.

"So, you don't have any pictures of Marlee?" I couldn't believe what I was hearing. That's why I've never seen a picture of my father, Bob. And why I'd never seen one of my sister.

Her eyes shifted down and then around. "I kept one," she said, her voice sounding like she was confessing a sin in a confessional booth.

Although we were alone in the house, she looked around to make sure no one else could see her. She walked over to her dresser and eased open the middle drawer, the one where she kept her sweaters. The scent of a lavender sachet wafted up—Mom put them in my drawers, too. I usually made a scene about them when she did it, but I kind of liked the smell—I just didn't want her to know I liked something so feminine.

She dug down into the drawer, underneath the sweaters, and pulled out a weathered photograph. "This one is from right before she got sick," she said. I could see Mom's eyes redden, and the corners of her eyes contract as if they might erupt at any minute. That was the closest I'd ever seen her come to crying. She handed the photo to me like it was one of those Catholic relics Dad kept in his dresser—a relic of the true cross or a piece of some saint's bone. They fascinated me and creeped me out at the same time.

The grainy photograph showed a young girl who looked to be about ten. She sat on a horse, in a Western saddle, her back straight, her hands loosely holding the reins, which rested comfortably on the saddle horn. She wore a long-sleeved plaid shirt and pants that in my era would have been jeans. Her slender legs and seat relaxed into the saddle, exuding experience and confidence. Her shoulder-length hair was dark and wavy, like my mother's.

Marlee the year before polio struck

From the look in the girl's eyes, I could almost hear her say, "Mom, hurry up and take the picture. I wanna ride." As I studied it, I wished I could be that comfortable on a horse.

Mom said, "She always loved horses." That's one of the few things I already knew about Marlee. "This picture is from right before she got sick," she repeated, and then she sat down on the bed, her shoulders slumped and her eyes closed.

I tried to see myself in this girl, my sister—my much older sister, though she was younger than I was then. It was like the picture froze her in time. Marlee, on her beautiful horse, with her dark-colored hair. Because it was a black and white photo, I couldn't tell the exact color, but I knew it didn't look like mine. Should I ask Mom about my red hair?

"I wished I'd known her," I said when I handed it back to her without asking anything else. She pressed the photo to her heart, then kissed it, and slid it back into the bottom of the dresser drawer. She glided the drawer shut with both hands, so it didn't make a sound. I wondered how many times she had opened and closed the drawer that way so she could look at her daughter's picture without one of us asking her what she was doing.

"I'm going to my room now," I announced, and before she turned around, I slipped out of their room and into mine. I eased the door shut as quietly as she had closed the dresser drawer and took a deep breath. I walked over to the record player and put on Bobbie Gentry's "Ode to Billie Joe." I liked bluesy and depressing songs, and this one, a ballad about a family secret, seemed appropriate for my mood.

I stood there and listened to the music for a minute and then collapsed on my bed. I grabbed my "Make Love Not War" pillow, a purchase from a headshop near the University of Arkansas in Fayetteville I'd recently snuck into with a friend. It was the '60s after all. In opposition to the sentiment expressed there, I gave the pillow a punch. *How could he have asked her to throw away pictures of her daughter? What's the matter with him?* My head felt like it was on fire. I punched the pillow again.

They were pictures of my sister and my father. Though my mother would never see the pictures again, I would never see them at all. In that moment, I felt Marlee's and Bob's loss in a way I'd never experienced before. I longed to learn their stories and to understand how they intersected with mine. But Dad had ripped their lives from the pages of our family's history and let them be blown away like leaves in a thunderstorm. Did he do it so I couldn't discover the truth, whatever that might be? And if so, what did he, did they, not want me to know?

This was the first time I remember feeling anger toward my father, and more than any other time in my life, I point to this moment as the time when I first recognized the destructive power of men's control of women's lives. Dad was not mean. He was just an ordinary man of his time. Mom complied with his demands because she understood that to be a requirement for their life together—for our life together.

It was in this discovery when secrets stopped feeling quite so harmless and the real questions began.

Mom never showed me the photo of Marlee again, and I never asked her to see it, although I would encounter it at another time, in another place. It was as if the photo and memories of Marlee were wrapped in a mummy waiting for someone to whisper their story to.

CHAPTER FIVE

Pardon

Although my parents were legally married in Colorado, that didn't matter to the Catholic Church. Because Dad was divorced, they lived in sin. That meant that as long as Dad's first wife was alive, the Church barred them from receiving the sacraments. As a result of this, my parents faced public humiliation at Mass every Sunday. I can still see them both, all dressed up in their Sunday best—Dad with a sport jacket and tie and Mom with a dress, white gloves, and a veil positioned gently over her graying hair. After kneeling through the consecration of the bread and wine, they would sit back in the pew, lift the kneeler up in front of them so people could pass, and wait. Others around them stood, made their way out of the pew, walked up to the communion rail with hands folded and heads bowed, took the host, which according to Catholic tradition had become the body of Christ, into their mouths, and returned to their seats.

After I turned seven and received my First Communion, I became more conscious of the stares. Before then, I sat back with them, played with my rosary or thumbed through the missal, while we waited together. But when I left them sitting there while I went up to receive Communion, I knew people wondered what they had done, why they sat back instead of rising up with their children. I kept my head bowed, not because I was praying, but so I couldn't see their stares. My parents' shame tainted me until my own soul felt dirty. When I returned to our pew, I prayed that God would forgive them, so I could be purified, too.

I imagine my mother experienced this mortification as penance for the sins she only ever hinted at to me. "If you only knew the things I've done," she would whisper to me when I got a little older. I knew not to ask what those things were. She would never have told me anyway. But I wondered. I liked to think that my mom was too good a person to do anything really bad, so I imagined that her shame had to have been the result of things done to her. But either way, I knew that she lived in a shroud of guilt and shame too thick for anything or anyone to penetrate.

One hot, summer day, an unexpected phone call freed my parents from their public embarrassment. I don't know who called. All I know is that when Dad hung up the phone, he told us that Aunt Betty, his first wife, had died. Although I hadn't seen Aunt Betty in years, I remembered and loved her, so the news made me sad. I couldn't judge my parents' mood, so I didn't know if it was OK to show them how I felt. My eleven-year-old self didn't understand the implications her death had on my parents' life. All I know is that the first Saturday morning after learning of Betty's death, my brother and I awoke to an empty house. That had never happened before.

"Mom and Dad are gone!" I exclaimed to my brother as I prodded him awake. "Where do you think they went?"

My distress was clearly not shared as he rolled over and mumbled, "Leave me alone," pulling the pillow over his head.

When Mom and Dad finally returned a couple of hours later, I was shocked to see that they were all dressed up. Clearly, they had been somewhere important. And without us! When I pushed Mom for more information, she replied with an unfamiliar brusqueness, "We just had some business to take care of."

Still not satisfied, I hovered over her as she squatted down and filed something away in the small metal file box they kept in the hall closet. That's when I glimpsed the words "Holy Matrimony" on the paper she tried to surreptitiously slip into a file folder. *What is that?* I thought. *Why is she putting away something to do with marriage?* I knew better than to press her any further. Being an inquisitive child, and already well-trained in the art of secrecy, I decided I'd investigate on my own at a later time.

I seized the first chance I had to see what she had hidden away. Later that same afternoon Mom ran out to the grocery store and Dad, pretending to be engrossed in a Notre Dame football game on TV, fell asleep on the couch. To be certain he was sleeping, I positioned myself on the floor between him and the TV and waited for him to tell me to move. When he didn't complain, I crept down the hallway to the linen closet.

I put my hand on the round, metal doorknob and gentled the right-side accordion door open. It squeaked, and I grimaced. I listened to make sure Dad hadn't awakened. A commercial blared from the TV, but I couldn't hear any other sounds. I turned back to the task at hand. Not wanting to risk more noise from opening the left-side door, I knelt down and crawled, the way an 11-year old child can, into the closet. I grabbed the top of the metal file and pulled the latch back that held it in place.

I found it right away—about halfway back, in a folder simply called *Papers*—a Certificate of Holy Matrimony from St. Vincent de Paul Catholic Church, dated that day. I maneuvered my body to see the certificate in the light from the hallway, and as I did my back banged against the inside of the closet door. Afraid I would get caught, my heart skipped a beat.

That didn't stop me though from sitting back on my knees and smiling. Even as a child, I knew what this meant. Mom and Dad were now married in the church. All censure was lifted—they could receive the sacraments again. They had been pardoned. As an earnest Catholic child, this meant everything to me.

I slid the paper back into the folder where I found it, wiggled out of the closet, glanced back down the hallway, and seeing it clear, guided the door back to a closed position. As I often did when I wanted time to myself, I left a note for Mom that I was out for a walk (Dad was still napping in front of the TV) and disappeared into the ravine behind our house. I made my way past the towering grape vines so strong we could swing across the ravine on them, down the steep rocky cliff, and to the crawdad creek that meandered through Lake Atalanta Park. There I sat on a rock, buried my bare feet in the mud, and being careful a crawdad wasn't poised to latch on to my toes, let the cool waters of the creek wash over them. I felt as if the Holy Spirit had come down from heaven and, just as my feet relaxed into the creek bed, washed all of our souls clean.

The next day, at Sunday Mass, I beamed with pride as Mom and Dad, for the first time as a married couple, rose with Jarrett and me to receive Holy Communion. Everything was OK now. We had become a holy family. No one would stare at us again.

That holy veil enveloped my family for a couple more years until, at the age of thirteen, I left the cocoon of my parents' house to spend the summer on my Aunt Babe and Uncle Paul's farm. On this, my first solo adventure, I discovered that my family's secrets might have permeated the thick walls meant to encase them.

Aunt Babe and Uncle Paul lived on a sixty-acre farm midway between Ann Arbor and Plymouth, Michigan. They had no children, although they seemed to love them, so I always wondered why they defied the norms of the day, especially the norms of other farmers, who typically depended on big families to help with all the chores.

Mom and Babe couldn't have been more different. Aunt Babe was older, taller—about 5'8" as compared to Mom's diminutive 5'2"—and much heavier. Mom was a well-mannered introvert who preferred refined indoor settings where, over morning coffee, she and her friends formed deep bonds with talk of husbands, kids, and the latest community happenings. Aunt Babe, on the other hand, was a gregarious extrovert. "Rough and Ready" she called herself—an epithet she embraced with vigor. Aunt Babe loved the outdoors, enjoyed getting dirty, and appreciated hard work. All things my mother deplored.

I favored Aunt Babe's approach to life. Going to the farm was my idea of heaven. I relished clawing my way to the top of the tumbling corn in the corn crib, taking walks with Uncle Paul to survey the back forty, picking wild raspberries and licking their juices off my fingers, and cutting bittersweet branches to decorate the kitchen table. I adored sitting down in the brooder house so that thousands of fluffy, yellow baby chicks could scramble over and around me. I devoured Aunt Babe's fried chicken—usually a hen she had slaughtered just that afternoon—mashed potatoes dripping with butter, and home-made strawberry-rhubarb pie. I squealed with delight when Aunt Babe offered Uncle Paul and me ice cream fresh from Cloverdale Dairy to accompany our TV watching at night. I breathed in the farm smells and breathed out the farm skies.

One afternoon, though, soon after I arrived for my long-anticipated summer visit, a simple question spoiled my farm adventure. Babe and I stopped at a corner market down the road, one of the many markets they serviced with their egg business. The owner was an old friend who greeted Babe warmly. When Babe introduced me as her niece, the owner, a gray-haired woman with a big smile, leaned over the counter and asked *the* question—the one I'd faced all my life.

"Where'd you get your red hair?"

Before the pre-programmed response tumbled from my mouth, "From my dad. My dad has red hair," my aunt snapped the answer right off my tongue. 'We don't know," she pronounced,

"Both her parents had black hair," and then whipped around and marched to the back of the store toward the milk cooler.

I stood there without uttering a word, busying myself with the penny candy in front of the counter. The afternoon sun reflected off the glass behind the bins, making the candy feel sticky to my hands. I wiped them on my shorts, but that didn't seem to help. *Why did she say that? That's not what we say.*

I walked over to a poster of the Marlboro Man hanging on the wall to wait for Aunt Babe to check out. I longed for the days when I used to wear a cowboy hat like his, so I could look tough and hide my red hair at the same time. Why did it seem like Aunt Babe was covering something up when she was really telling the truth? At least what I'd been told was the truth.

When we got into the truck to head back to the farm, I didn't ask her about it. Nor did I ask her when we sat down to dinner with Uncle Paul. I didn't want to upset her, and I had a feeling that bringing it up again might. When my month on the farm ended, I returned home full of even more questions and a growing uneasiness that something about my family didn't add up.

I'd never actually seen a picture of my father. That, in and of itself, was strange. Mom had told me why she didn't have any—that Dad had made her get rid of all her photos of Bob and Marlee, so he could be our only dad. On one of the rare occasions when Mom mentioned him, she told me Bob had black hair, like hers, confirming what Aunt Babe told the storekeeper. So, if I didn't share his hair color, I wondered if I looked like Bob in other ways. *Did I have his eyes? His build?* The questions just prompted other questions that I didn't know how to answer.

As I grew up, I noticed other threads that didn't belong in the book that was our family's story. But the question: "where did my red hair really come from?" haunted me, the way a reader might fold the corner of a page in a mystery novel that holds a clue to solving the crime.

Part Two

CHAPTER SIX

Science and the Art of Persuasion

A lot of adopted kids begin to ask questions when they first learn about genetics in high school biology. I was no different. Despite the fact it was now a stunning silver gray, I knew Mom originally had black hair. From the one photo I had seen, I figured Marlee had black hair, too. The photo was in black and white, so I couldn't tell for certain, but it was definitely much darker than mine. If Mom's first husband and my supposed father, Bob, had black hair, too, where did my red hair come from? Was it possible for two black-haired parents to have two red-haired kids?

"Theoretically, yes," my 10th grade biology teacher responded when I asked, "but it's rare."

I swallowed hard at the answer, but I didn't let on the reason for my question. Although some kids began to question whether the parents who were raising them gave birth to them, I seriously began to wonder whether the father who was raising me, the father who legally adopted me, was actually my biological father. That would be weird, I knew, but my love of mysteries encouraged me to ask the questions.

My best friend (and lab partner) Cindy and I would spend hours spinning tales about how it might have been possible for Mom to get pregnant twice by a man who was not her husband (I had no doubt that Jarrett was my full brother. Despite our 21-month age difference, we could have been twins). It was great fodder for conversation for two high school sophomores as we explored the meaning of fidelity and infidelity in the teenage relationships that exploded around us. Cindy thought it was a riot—the idea that parents had exciting, secret lives. We laughed and joked about every soap-opera-like possibility. Although I played along, it always left me with a gnawing feeling in my stomach that wouldn't go away even after I left Cindy's house to go home to mine.

I guess you could say I was a late bloomer. By the time we were in 10th grade, Cindy, along with every other girl I knew, was all about boys. I had no interest in dating. I'd survived junior high without a boyfriend, or, for that matter, even a date. By tenth grade, the pressure grew.

If my parents were alive today, they would deny this, but by the time I turned 15, a year *before* I could legally drive without a licensed driver accompanying me, they let me take the station wagon whenever I wanted to go out. It was the only blue car, or should I say, not-green car, I ever remember my family having as a kid. In those days, stations wagons were big hunkers, and this one, probably a 1967 or '68 Chevy Impala, was no exception. Not exactly a teenager's dream car. But it was a car, and that was all that mattered to me.

On a typical Friday or Saturday night, Cindy and I drove the eight miles from Rogers to Bentonville (best known today as the home of Wal-Mart Corporation) to look for boys. "They have cuter boys in Bentonville," Cindy would say, and off we'd go. There was this one boy, James, that Cindy particularly liked. I remember his name because James Taylor's album *Sweet Baby James* had just come out and Cindy was convinced it was just for her. Typically, we'd meet up with James at the Bentonville Bowl (classy date, I know). While Cindy and James would go to his car to make out, I would sit in the station wagon and wait. When they were done, I would dutifully drive her back home while she described, in remarkable detail, everything they did.

When Cindy became consumed with boys and dating and started pushing me to do the same, I found another friend—one who wasn't as boy crazy—and started spending more time with her. Cindy and I still got together, and we still talked about boys, but I stopped driving her to meet them. I don't remember how that changed, only that it did, and for a while, it worked balancing two separate friendships: one with Cindy and one with my new friend Beth.

Beth had just moved to Rogers and needed a friend. She liked boys but had lots of other interests too, like books and travel. Because of that, I felt like I could contribute something to the conversation. For a few months, the pressure to date subsided. Until I introduced Beth to Sally.

Sally was a casual friend who I hung out with on occasion in junior high. She could be described as kind of a wild kid. Her father owned a clothing store downtown, so everyone knew the family. They also had more money than most of us—certainly more than we did. Sally drove too, but not a clunky station wagon like me. Sally drove a late-model Oldsmobile Cutlass. She loved to drive fast, but her dad must have known that and had some type of control put on it that didn't let her go over 70. That really pissed her off, but it didn't stop her from pushing the car to its limits. Her family owned a lot of undeveloped property located off dirt roads outside of town. She loved to race down those roads—the dust enveloping us in a cloud so thick she'd have to turn on her windshield wipers to see the way forward. When we reached any place where a car could pull off and hide in the trees, Sally would note it as a possible parking spot (with a boy, that is).

I don't remember how it happened, but somehow, someday, for some reason, I invited Beth to go with Sally and me on one of these adventures. Sally said OK, even though she didn't know Beth. The next thing I knew, they stopped returning my calls, stopping inviting me to go to the movies with them, stopped speaking to me at school. I felt like a jilted lover who never saw it coming. I'd already been missing Cindy, and now I'd lost Beth, too.

I responded by shutting myself into my room whenever I was home, which was all the time I wasn't in school or church. I'd put on a record, lay on the bed, and stare out the window. Sometimes I'd read. Sometimes I'd grab a hairbrush to use as a microphone and watch myself in the mirror as I lip-synced the Billboard Top 40. In those moments, I imagined myself a sexy (male) pop star with an adoring woman-friend watching from the wings. It never dawned on me that this would be considered unusual. I knew nothing about alternative lifestyles. I just knew boys and blondes had to have more fun.

I emerged from my room only to eat, and since my favorite TV series *Star Trek* had gone off the air earlier that year, even TV couldn't entice me to stay out in the public areas of the house after I completed my obligatory chores cleaning up the kitchen.

I didn't know then why I didn't like doing the things other girls my age did. I didn't know why I got bored spending all my time hearing my friends talk about boys. I didn't know then that my life would take a different course from theirs.

As I look back on that tumultuous sophomore year, three scenes reverberate in my memory as clearly as if I'd just watched them in a movie. They each played a critical role in my next step toward independence.

Scene One

I'm in Speech class—sitting in a school desk, my feet curled up under the seat, closed books on the desktop, my head down, my eyes staring at the floor. My brother's friend, Barbara, comes into class and sits at the desk next to me. I barely notice her and don't acknowledge her. She leans across the aisle toward me. "Jarrett says you've been depressed lately; do you want to talk about it?"

I feel heat rising in my face. I'm immediately self-conscious. As a redhead with fair skin, I know that if I'm feeling heat, my face is showing it. I turn my head the other way. My heart is racing. In that split second, I wonder what vibes I'm putting off that even my brother, who barely notices me, had perceived my mood. I wrap my arms tighter around me. I'm mortified that anyone could break through my shields to know how I'm feeling.

"No, I'm fine," I say quickly, without looking at her. "But thank you," I add, almost at a whisper.

"OK," she replies, as she pulls herself back to her desk. "But if you ever want to talk about anything, give me a call."

I still don't look at her. I don't respond. Relief sweeps over me when Mr. Smalley calls us to order and class begins.

Barbara and I never talked about it. I never talked to anyone about what had happened. Mom noticed that I didn't hang out with Beth and Sally anymore, that I didn't hang out with anyone anymore, but she didn't push. No one pushed. I imagined an invisible deflector shield around me like the one that encircles the Starship Enterprise that I didn't allow anyone to breach.

Scene Two

Mom and I are in the kitchen. She's screaming at me about something I don't remember. I'm startled by the intensity of her anger. She starts smacking me, first on the arm, and then my face, something she had never, ever done before. I flee to my room. She chases me there. I roll over my bed and wedge myself between the bed and wall to get away from her. She climbs on the bed and slaps at me with both hands. She mostly misses. After a few futile attempts to reach me, she leaves me lying there, slamming my bedroom door on her way out.

I stay on the floor between the bed and wall for several minutes, long enough for my shock to subside, for my heart to slow down, to feel safe. By the time I get up, I can hear Mom in the kitchen.

I know she's preparing dinner for my brother who'll be home from football practice soon. By the time he arrives, she will have composed herself so that everything will appear normal to him. She would never want him to see her that way.

I stay in my room. I wish I could cry but, just like Mom, I never cry. Instead, I grab my Teddy Bear, Timmy, the one I've had since I was two, and bite hard on his ear before throwing him across the room. Timmy crashes into the corner next to my desk.

"I have to get out of here," I mouth to the image in the mirror.

Scene Three

I hurry out to the mailbox, as I have done every day since I carefully typed a letter on the old Smith-Corona typewriter Aunt Babe gave me, folded the letter neatly, and put it in an envelope, which I then licked, stamped, and prayed over before dropping in a mailbox near my high school. I know a reply will take a couple of weeks, maybe longer, but that doesn't stop me from checking.

I pause before opening the mailbox. Today will be the day. I know it. It's been just over two weeks, and the waiting has become unbearable. Before pulling the mailbox door open, I invoke the name of my only true friend, Jesus.

"Jesus, let it be here, please. The letter I'm waiting for. The one that can free me from this life."

I spy it even though it's covered by credit card bills from Dad's most recent business trip. I slide the envelope out and leave the others there. I have what I came for. I stare at it as I run my fingers over the embossed name on the return address, St. Joseph's Academy, Adrian, Michigan.

The envelope is thick and heavy like it holds the keys to heaven. I run into the house, letting the front screen door slam behind me.

"Any mail?" mom asks as I slither past her.

"Oh, I forgot to check. I'll get it later," I lie as I steal into my room. I close the door behind me, press my back against it, and slide down to the floor. I tear open the envelope. A full-color brochure falls out with a photo of the three-story brick building I remember from a visit there when I was little.

Situated at the end of a series of connected buildings that include the Adrian Dominican Motherhouse, St. Joseph's Academy houses an elementary day school and a high school boarding school. Both schools are all girls. The photo floods my mind with memories—of nuns draped in white and black walking serenely among stately old buildings and towering oak trees toward the grotto where the Blessed Virgin Mary awaited their arrival. My dad's sister, my favorite aunt, Sister Patricia Anne—Aunt Millie to us—who died of cancer five years earlier, walked with them in the center of the group. A feeling of peace and belonging rushes over me, just like it did when I saw the nuns there. I must have only been seven or eight at the time, but I'd never forgotten that feeling. If I play my cards right, this envelope will be my ticket back there—and out of here.

All I have to do to go there instead of returning to Rogers Senior High School is convince my parents to send me.

I don't remember all the arguments I made to persuade them that they should send me to boarding school in Michigan, especially since Jarrett was graduating high school and leaving for the U.S. Naval Academy in a couple of months.

I know I worked on Dad first. In fact, I don't remember talking with Mom about it at all. The arguments I remember making, probably because they were the ones that worked, started with telling Dad how much I loved Aunt Millie and how much I missed her. Playing on the prejudice that I knew both Mom and Dad had toward southerners, I then told him I needed to leave Arkansas and go back up north so I could get a good education. I told him that I didn't like being in public school and that I'd already taken all the classes I wanted to take at Rogers High. I needed a more challenging school.

Whether they agreed with me or not, something worked, because rather than completing my high school education in Rogers, my parents drove me over 800 miles north to attend St. Joseph's Academy for my junior and senior high school years.

Mom later claimed it was the worst decision she ever made in her life. That's because it was there that I found out why I didn't like boys.

CHAPTER SEVEN

Forbidden Passageways

When I arrived at St. Joseph's Academy five years after seeing the iconic 1966 movie *The Trouble with Angels*, which depicted a comedic version of life in a Catholic girls school, I had little idea what to expect. I knew there would be nuns. I knew there would be girls and, most importantly, no boys. I knew there would be books and classes and studying. I knew there would be church and religion courses. I knew my class would be much smaller than it was at Rogers High School—thirty students compared to several hundred. But would there be devious pranks designed to outsmart the sisters like those shown in the movie? Would the girls be as boy crazy as those at my current school? Would I like it there? I didn't know. All I knew was that it was worth the risk, or at least I prayed it would be.

Most of the students in my class had attended the Academy since freshman year—a couple had been attending as day students from the community since they were in first grade. But a few, like me, were new. Some students who'd been around for a while struggled to adjust to jarring changes, like nuns who no longer wore habits, more relaxed school uniforms, and field trips to see two radical Broadway productions, *Jesus Christ Superstar* and *Godspell*, while others, along with many of us who were new, relished in them. The times they were a-changin'.

Of the thirty-six students in my junior and senior years combined, six students had been sent to the U.S. from Central and South American countries to develop their cultural competency before returning home to resume their lives. Some spoke fluent English, a few did not. Four of the students were Black. I had never met people of other races and ethnicities before, so this was all new to me.

My hometown, Rogers, Arkansas, publicly prided itself on being a White community, a documented sundown town (though I didn't know that term then), where people of color were warned to be out of town by sundown or face dire consequences. Fitting into this diverse educational and living environment presented new challenges to this awkward, shy girl trying to find her way in a new world.

Because my parents were not from Arkansas, I'd never developed the "hillbilly" accent of the people born there. And yet, I soon discovered that I did not speak like the other White Michigan girls in my class. My speech had a twang that was decidedly not northern. I found myself listening closely and doing my best to mimic what I heard, all to fit in. My mother taught me well. Losing what little accent I had became an obsession. Above all else, I wanted to connect with those girls most like me—the smart, mostly well-behaved White girls.

At the same time, I had two years of Spanish behind me and had even taken a class trip to Mexico in my sophomore year, so I enjoyed talking with the "Spanish" girls and learning about their countries and their cultures.

The Black girls in my class were harder for me to bond with. In retrospect, I know that although I didn't grow up in racist household, my town's racism had infected me. Most strikingly, I didn't believe that the Black students were as smart as the White girls (a belief I now know showed that I was the stupid one), so I didn't treat them the same. By the spring of my first year there, I acted on this unconscious racism by challenging the girl who had served as class president for the previous three years.

Sheryl was a Black girl from Detroit who touted her association with the Black Panthers and presented herself with an air of certainty and sophistication. There was no doubt she was smart, but I figured, by luck of genetics, I was smarter. Soon after I announced that I was running, Sheryl dropped out. It never occurred to me to wonder why—then, or even after I'd won—and I didn't ask. Chances are she wouldn't have told me anyway. I was not someone she had a reason to trust. It would take me a number of years to learn and understand what it meant for a White person to step back and support BIPOC (Black, Indigenous, people of color) leadership.

By the spring of my senior year, I'd proven myself as a dependable, responsible leader to many (most?) of the students and faculty.

Michelle changed everything.

Except for a few who lived too far away to travel for such a short break, most Academy students had gone home or to a relative's or friend's house for Easter vacation that year. Michelle and I were seniors, only a month or so from graduation, so while the nuns who managed the dorm tended to the younger kids, we were pretty much left to our own devices. Michelle lived only a couple hours from school, so I don't remember why she couldn't go home. I can only suspect that she stayed because she had plans unrelated to Christ's resurrection.

At some point each day, Michelle and I would make our way through the tunnels from our dorm to the Motherhouse for hand bell choir rehearsal, an important piece of the upcoming Holy Week services. Some students were afraid of the tunnels that laced their way like rabbit burrows from one end of campus, which housed the Montessori through high school academy, under the Adrian Dominican Motherhouse, to Siena Heights College (now University). But I loved them. And even though we weren't supposed to use them, I relished any excuse to take them somewhere, anywhere. Each time I slunk into them, I pretended I was on a spy mission, had secret access to a palace, or was a criminal mastermind about to rob precious jewels from a stodgy museum.

To get to rehearsal, Michelle and I slipped down the long, forbidden passageway, past the giant salt bin (the purpose of which I never understood), around a dark corner, through the nun's dining room, up the back stairs, and then up one more set of stairs to arrive in the choir loft above Holy Rosary Chapel, never once having to brave whatever foul weather might be churning outside. There we'd meet Sister Magdalena and other nuns poised to play their bells in celebration of Jesus's resurrection.

If you've never played hand bells, you might not know that it's not as easy as it might appear. First, it's important to understand that each bell rings a different note, so you might be assigned responsibility for playing little bells that produce high notes on the scale, or big bells that produce deep, resonating sounds. In essence, all the members of the bell choir join together to become one instrument with each person playing one or two notes in concert with others to make a melody.

Ringing them is not a simple matter of holding up the bell and hitting it incessantly like Sister Ursula, portress in *The Trouble with Angels* did. She used the bell to call the students to chapel, to meals, and awaken them every morning at 6:00 am. I'm sure if we had had a Sister Ursala, I wouldn't be clamoring to play in the bell choir. But these were very different kinds of bells.

It took me a while to learn the correct technique, including the proper way to hold the bell, which is straight up but leaning a little bit back toward your body, while maintaining a good grasp on it so the handbell doesn't fly across the room as you ring it. To sound each bell, you draw a circle—down, forward, and then up and around. The clapper is supposed to hit on the downstroke and, if you bring it back properly, it doesn't ring errantly on the upstroke—a definite no-no.

Once the bell sounds, it typically needs to be damped by touching it to your body or, if you're picking up another bell, laying it on the table. In this way, members can ring all the notes in whatever piece of music the choir is playing.

I was not gifted with tremendous rhythm. Despite that, at thirteen, I took up guitar—it was the '60s after all—and I got to be a decent rhythm player. I played at parties with others who were typically better than me, and at guitar masses where I would accompany a choir belting out the latest post-Vatican II (aka modern) hymn.

But rhythm guitar is very forgiving, especially compared to handbells. If you're a little slow in changing chords on a guitar, most people don't notice much, especially when accompanying a church choir or after a few beers with semi-intoxicated vocalists. But when your single note in a bell choir chimes early, late, too softly, loudly, or long people notice. Even though I'd become a class leader at the Academy, I didn't like standing out. To play my notes at the exact right moment, with the right force, and for the right length, I had to practice—hard.

I still cringe when I remember the poorly timed notes emanating from the bells in my hands. Michelle, on the other hand, a lithe brunette with a knowing smile and confident air, rang her bells in perfect time, never missing a beat. I couldn't help but admire her gift. She did her best to help me, encourage me, and teach me, but I struggled even under her attentive tutelage.

I don't know if it was the bells that brought us closer. All I remember is that during this time, when other students were gone and the sounds of bells echoed in my head, Michelle and I found ourselves sitting on a shabby old couch in a little used room on the first floor of our dorm sharing a contraband bottle of Boone's Farm Apple Wine.

I remember the dreary light emanating from the hall. I remember the distance closing between us. I remember kicking the now empty bottle on the floor at our feet. I remember the touch of a butterfly on a delicate sunflower. I remember tingling.

This was not my first kiss. My first kiss was with a boy. His name was Kevin. We dated for a few months and went to the junior prom together. That's where we kissed. And kissed. We both discovered that we loved kissing. In my senior year, a few months after the prom, I got a call that Kevin was in the hospital. The psychiatric wing. Kevin had attempted to take his own life.

Only later, when I was in college, did Kevin invite me to join him at a gay bar in Ann Arbor. That's how he came out to me. He died a short time after that. I never learned if he died by suicide or, if, given it was the 1980s, AIDS was the culprit. I just know I'll always remember those first passionate kisses—kisses that eventually led me to drinking a bottle of cheap wine with a girl on a raggedy couch in a Catholic girls school dormitory.

This kiss was nothing like Kevin's. I couldn't believe what I was feeling. All I wanted was more. All I wanted was her.

Ironically, although this kiss changed my life in ways I couldn't even comprehend at the time, I don't remember when we moved beyond kissing to making love. Being one of the few kids who insisted on and had been afforded a private dorm room, we had the luxury of closing my door, and despite the fact that it wasn't lockable, shutting everyone else out. Michelle would sneak into my room late at night and we would frolic around until dawn was about to break. Then she'd creep back to her four-bed dorm room so we could greet the day without anybody being wiser. Or so we liked to believe.

Clichés aside, I was in heaven. As far as I recall, I had no concept of what it meant to be a lesbian. I don't think I'd ever heard the word. I might be fooling myself when I say that. It's possible that I knew more than I remember. But I do know that I was in love, that it felt right to me, and nothing could be better than that.

I knew not to talk about it though. Even if I had words for what we were doing, I knew what was happening between Michelle and me had to remain a secret. I don't know how I knew that. I don't know if Michelle and I talked about it. Surely, we must have plotted our clandestine rendezvous—one of which took place in that giant salt bin hidden in the restricted tunnels to the Motherhouse. All I know is that being well-schooled in secret-keeping by my parents, I fell right into my own undercover world. While other girls my age boasted about their handsome boyfriends, I smiled and didn't say a thing about my love life.

When I tell other lesbians that I went to an all-girls high school, they often get dreamy-eyed at the thought of it. Although it took me until the spring of my senior year to live up to their imaginations, our antics that year far exceeded anything Haley Mills tried in *The Trouble with Angels*.

Whatever I knew or didn't know, I recognized what we were doing would not be viewed positively by the nuns whose trust and respect I'd earned. The question was, would they catch on? It didn't take me long to find out.

CHAPTER EIGHT

Holy Outing

I knew something was wrong the moment I heard my mother's voice, a blend of despair and disappointment that sent a chill down my spine. A few short weeks after I found love, I graduated from high school, returned home to Rogers, got a job waiting tables at the local Holiday Inn, and, while anticipating my return to college in the North, spent my time pining for Michelle.

One afternoon after my shift, Mom summoned me into the family room. The air conditioner was no match for the relentless Arkansas sun as it beat down through the picture window at that time of day. The family room was the last place I wanted to be, but this was a rare request and it didn't feel like challenging it would be in my best interest.

I had no context for, or experience with, serious conversations with Mom—we just didn't have them. When she was upset, she didn't talk about it or, except for that one time when she chased me into my room, even show it. She had taught me—expected me—to do the same. I sat down on the hassock in front of the chair she was in. In retrospect, this wasn't the smartest move. It's hard to come across as self-assured or defiant, depending on what would be required, sitting on a hassock.

"Sister Barbara called me," she began.

"She did?" I was as much intrigued as surprised. "When? What for?"

"Last month. That's not important." She waved her hand in the air dismissively. "What's important is that she's concerned about you." A look passed over Mom's face that I'd never seen before. Distant, defeated, like she'd just lost a precious pearl, one she knew she would never get back.

Uh, oh. This was not good. "Last month?" I asked to give myself time to think. That meant she called before graduation—and I'm just hearing about it now?

My mind flashed back to Lumen Chapel. Graduation had just concluded. Michelle and I were standing outside with other graduates in our caps and gowns. Parents milled about with looks of pride and probably some relief on their faces. Dad handed me a greeting card. I could tell the envelope held something more than a card. I slipped open the seal and two photos fell out. As I reached down to pick them up, a blazing orange car sitting in our driveway back home came into view. My eyes grew wide. I choked. I couldn't believe what I was seeing.

"This is for me?" I stammered as I scooped up the photos, certain the images might disappear, and the car along with them, if I didn't ask fast enough.

"Yes," Dad said. "We thought you'd like it."

Like it? I loved it and I hadn't even seen it yet. My own car! In my favorite color. I couldn't wait to get home now.

"It's a 1973 Pontiac Ventura Hatchback," he went on. "Pretty spiffy."

Pretty spiffy indeed!

Now that I was home and had claimed the beautiful car as my own, I wished I was driving it instead of sitting here on a hassock in the family room with mom.

"Sister Barbara said you were involved in, in," the words caught in her throat. "in an unsavory relationship with another girl—with that Michelle girl." The way she said, "that Michelle girl," I could see the words spill out of her mouth, down her blouse, and onto the carpet.

I didn't react—at least not externally. Inside, I felt like I'd just been run over by my new car.

"Are you a," she closed her eyes and swallowed hard. I wondered if she might throw up. "a homosexual?" She spit the words out and then turned her head and locked her eyes on the floor, bracing for my answer to slap her in the face.

I didn't understand her question. I had no idea what the word even meant.

My mind flashed back to a conversation I'd had with Sister Barbara a few weeks earlier. She called me into her choir room and, while seated at the grand piano, her fingers poised over the keys as if she were about to start playing, she charged, "You and Michelle are spending too much time together." She relaxed her fingers resting them on the keyboard but didn't look up at me before adding. "You need to do a better job of guarding your reputation. People are talking."

Each word hit me like a staccato note in the refrain of the new piece she'd introduced us to earlier that day in my third period choir class.

My heart ached at the thought of someone talking about me, telling Sister Barbara bad things about me—and Sister Barbara thinking bad things about me.

I backed up and tried to hide behind the piano's lid so she couldn't see my face.

I asked what people were saying, but she wouldn't tell me. "Just be careful," she warned, as she finally began to play—silky notes belying the stiffness in her voice. I backed out of the room and let notes of some classical piece I didn't recognize guide me through the door.

I reached the hall, eased the door shut behind me, and leaned against it. I closed my eyes and took in, and then let out, a deep breath. I didn't know whether to be filled with shame or anger. I didn't get into trouble like that. What right did she have to tell me who I could be friends with? What did she mean by "guarding my reputation?" I knew one thing—her warning wasn't going to change how I felt about Michelle.

I left that conversation resolute but wary. I told Michelle we needed to lay low for a while, but it didn't change how I felt. I was in love for the first time in my life and couldn't imagine how anyone could think it was wrong.

Sister Barbara hadn't used the word homosexual when she talked to me but that must have been the word she used when she called Mom. I don't think Mom would have come up with it on her own.

I can't remember how I answered Mom's question. I do remember how devastated I was when our conversation was over. What had been natural and beautiful to me was something Sister Barbara had told me was ruining my reputation, and now Mom said it was something I should be ashamed of. Something dirty. Sinful. Sick.

"What have I done wrong?" she cried. "You need to go see the priest," she pleaded. "Promise me you'll go see the priest."

I wouldn't. I couldn't. What would I say to him?

"I should never have let you go to that school," she said shaking her head as if admitting defeat.

When the conversation ended, instead of hopping on my bike like I always had as a kid when things got tense at home, I jumped into my spirited, brand new orange car. When I turned the key in the ignition and backed out of the driveway, I was in control, on my own, free to go and do what I wanted. Today, however, I felt more like I'd been caught in the pistons and battered around before being spit out onto the driveway.

Luckily, I didn't have to think about where I wanted to go because I wasn't thinking at all. My brain felt dull and dense, like a rubber eraser. I pulled into a parking spot on W. Poplar Street, slipped the car into park, put a quarter in the meter, and ran up the stairs, two at a time.

When I flung open the heavy, white wood and glass doors, I knew I was safe. The Rogers Hough Memorial Library—my library—was like an old friend. I'd spent countless hours here extracting, no, divining, the secrets of the universe in this magical place. The library held the answers to every question, the solution to every problem. Sometimes, I'd methodically search the card catalog and then follow its cryptic code like a treasure map to the exact spot where a book was shelved. Other times, I'd roam the stacks until I stumbled upon something that captured my imagination. Either way, when I found a book that interested me, I'd plop down on the floor and read. Somewhere in here, I could find out about this sinful, shameful sickness that everyone seemed so upset about. I was sure of it.

I proceeded directly to the card catalog. I quickly browsed the labels until my eyes zeroed in on the drawer that held the H's, GA-HZ. That's it. I slid it open, lifted the long, over-stuffed drawer out of the wooden cabinet, and placed it on the table. I scanned the room to make sure no one I knew was around, that no one would sneak up behind me to see what I was doing. This was a small town, after all, and chances were someone I knew, or who knew me, was in here, too.

When I determined it was safe, I rummaged through the cards, some with book titles on them, some with authors, some with subjects. I focused on the subjects. Ha, Hi, Ho. Homeostasis, Homosapien, Honeybees. Wait a minute. I must have missed it. I went through the cards backwards, one card at a time. Nothing. Neither "homosexual" nor "homosexuality" was listed. I was sure it would be in here.

I fought back a growing sense of despair. I certainly wasn't going to ask the librarian, Mrs. Osgood. She had moved from Plymouth to Rogers with Daisy, just like we did. She'd been our librarian in Michigan and now she was our librarian here. She was a kind, old lady, but I knew enough not to ask her about this. I slid the card catalog drawer back into place, fingers lingering on the metal drawer pull as if I could will the card I needed to be there. I tried to think of some other word I could look for, but I didn't know any others. The word hummed in my head begging for meaning.

I moved over to the dictionary, which sat on a pedestal in the center of the first-floor study area. It might not have the answer, but at least it might have a clue, and I knew that with enough clues you could solve any mystery—at least my old friends, The Three Investigators, could. To get to the H's, I lifted what must have been several hundred pages from the right side of the gargantuan tome to the left.

I ran my finger down the page. There it was: Homosexual. "a man with sexual desire for another man." I stood there and stared. It didn't say anything about me—about love, tenderness, or the sweet caress of Michelle's lips. Nor did it say anything about mental illness, sin, or the shame I was supposed to feel for the love I experienced with Michelle. Nothing in the dictionary definition applied to me at all.

I flipped the pages to the M's so no one would see where I'd been looking and collapsed into a chair at a nearby table. What now? I couldn't remember feeling so alone. Even my library had betrayed me. I wished I could call Michelle. She was with her sister, an Adrian Dominican nun, at her sister's convent in Chicago, so there would be no way I would get through to her. I had no one I could talk to. No one who would understand.

The summer progressed as slowly as a walking stick climbing up my favorite oak tree at the end of our driveway. I worked as much as I could to avoid being at home. I scouted out pay phones in obscure locations around town so Michelle and I could sneak in an occasional call. When I was home, I stalked the mail truck so I could grab any letters she sent me before Mom checked the mail. I even arranged for Michelle to send mail by General Delivery to the next town over only to have the postmistress question my mom about why I was getting mail in Bentonville. I felt invaded, persecuted—and infatuated. I couldn't get enough—of Michelle or the intrigue! My parents' secret-keeping paled in relation to my own deviousness.

I had to wait until I returned to Michigan for college, though, to finally read something about the real meaning of homosexuality. I was in a friend's dorm room when I spotted a book on her shelf. I swallowed hard and screwed up my courage to ask, "Can I, um, borrow that book, um, about Sappho?" I wasn't sure who Sappho was, but I'd heard enough to make me curious.

My friend laughed, "It's not about Sappho. It's about us. Of course, you can borrow it."

Sappho Was a Right-On Woman: A Liberated View of Lesbianism by Sidney Abbott and Barbara Love was one of the first books written by a lesbian, about lesbians, and thankfully, the first book I ever read about homosexuality.

I hadn't realized how sheltered I'd been all those years growing up in Rogers. I knew nothing about lesbians, or the "gay" lifestyle, or even why the Church considered it a sin. The topic, like so many others, had been erased in my household. From this book, I learned about women who'd found happiness and were living fulfilling lives in love with other women. This book described exactly how I felt and didn't make it sound sick or sinful at all.

I'd found my people. Now I just had to figure out how not to hide who I was so I could be one of them.

CHAPTER NINE

Unlikely Sources

The oversized envelope caught my eye the moment I pushed through the double doors to my dorm. The thin manila parcel pressed against my door as if the wind had blown it there and refused to let go. I'd hoped to lose myself in *Lord of the Flies* before dinner. Despite the fact that it was required reading, the novel's premise fascinated me and offered a welcome escape from a day of classes. But as soon as I saw the envelope, I knew my plans had changed.

I picked up the packet and held it in my hands like one would embrace a precious family heirloom. I pushed open my door, dropped my book bag on the floor, and crawled up on my bed, all the while not taking my eyes off the envelope. The return address popped off the page like a neon sign. State of Michigan Vital Records Office. I could feel my pulse quickening. My apprehension about opening it surprised me. Were the records contained in this envelope really vital, and if so, to whom?

This would be the first time I'd seen my birth certificate. Certainly, this official document would tell me the truth. Seeing Robert L. Smith listed as my birth father would put to rest any nagging questions I had. I would have legal proof of who my "real" father was.

I stared at it in what felt like suspended animation. It's just a birth certificate, for God's sake. I sucked in a breath, slid my finger under the flap, and carefully opened the envelope. When I pulled out the embossed paper, I ran my fingers over the back of the raised stamp before unfolding it.

As soon as I looked at the page, I knew something was wrong. A date stamped at the bottom caught my eye. Oct 25, 1962. That didn't make sense. I was in second grade in 1962. Why was my birth certificate issued seven years after I was born?

I scanned up the page. There, under Father, wasn't Robert L. Smith, the man my mother told me was our father, but Norman W. Marquis, the man who adopted me. What? How could he be listed as my father on my birth certificate?

Just as Dad did in making Mom throw away her photographs of Bob, history had again been rewritten. This time by the State—on my official, verified, certified, recorded, and filed birth certificate.

Or had it?

Maybe the State had corrected an error it made at the time of my birth. Maybe Norm really was my father. If the State erased all evidence of the role Bob played in my life, maybe it was because he hadn't played a role. I sat back on my bed and let the pillows comfort me.

How was I going to learn who I was if all I discovered was that more evidence had been compromised? If even the State colluded with my parents to obfuscate the truth? A feeling of despair came over me as I realized I had little hope of ever knowing who my father really was. This document wasn't going to tell me anything.

I would have to piece the puzzle of my family together on my own and, in that moment, when even the State conspired against me, it seemed like an impossible task to a teenage girl with her own secrets to keep.

A couple years after I saw my birth certificate for the first time, my mom's sister, Wilma, who we called Aunt Babe, sorted through a large box of photographs at her dining room table. I'd come for the weekend. Just like when I was younger, I loved visiting the farm, and because it was only an hour's drive from school, I made it a regular part of my college routine.

Although we often spent my time there outside with the peacocks, geese, and their horde of cats, on this day, roaring thunderstorms kept us in. Aunt Babe pushed a stack of photos across the large walnut table where we'd held family gatherings when, as a kid, my family made the trek from Arkansas back to Michigan to visit our relatives.

"You might want these," she said, without looking up.

I pulled the stack toward me. I immediately recognized Marlee from the grainy horse picture I'd seen a few years earlier hidden in my mother's dresser. I can imagine I let out an audible gasp. I know my eyes widened because I can feel that happening as I write about it.

In many of these pictures, Marlee is younger than the ten- or eleven-year-old girl who sat confidently astride a horse, although a copy of that photo was there, too. Some photos showed an infant, others a toddler, and still others a precocious child of five or six. In every picture, I saw the slender, dark-haired woman who would become my mother cuddle this child in her arms, stand beside her holding her hand, or push her along in a baby carriage. The love they felt for one another infused the images so that each photo felt warm in my hands.

When a slender man with dark hair, sporting a white t-shirt, appeared in multiple shots, I figured out who he was, but I asked anyway, "Is this Bob?" The hesitancy in my voice was unmistakable. I had no difficulty calling him Bob. Uncle Norm had become Dad, so it just seemed right to call Bob by his name. My hesitation came not from using his name but from realizing how little I looked like him.

"Um hum," she replied, staying engrossed in the photos before her. And then, after a pause, she asked, "Haven't you ever seen him before?"

"No," I replied. "Mom doesn't have any photos of him." I answered with a nonchalance that ironically felt forced. I didn't add that my dad made her get rid of them. I figured Aunt Babe could surmise that.

The three of them looked like a family. Their hair, their skin coloring, their dress. They belonged together. I wondered if, held up against a similar photo of the same woman with a different man and two red-haired children, I would feel the same.

Aunt Babe said I could have the photos. I scarfed them up like they were the Hershey's chocolate squares she always had stocked for me in the cabinet behind where I sat.

"I don't know what's on these," she said as she pushed a few rolls of 8 mm film toward me. "But you might find something there worth watching." I snatched them up, too.

When I got back to my apartment, I didn't look at them again—the photos or the videos. Just having them in my possession felt like I'd robbed a bank. As anxious as I was to know about my family's history, every time I got closer, I felt myself pull back, afraid of what I might discover. I couldn't help but feel that way now. I wanted to know, but what if I learned more than I bargained for?

I stashed the photos and the film away in a cardboard box and slid the box on to the top shelf in my closet. Someday, I'd look at them. Someday, I'd pull the photos out and study the facial features of this family that wasn't mine. Someday, I'd borrow an 8 mm movie projector, thread the delicate film through the reels, and watch this family come to life.

But not now. As much as I yearned for the truth, I felt in my bones that I wasn't ready to know.

Although I still hadn't re-examined the treasure trove of photos or watched the home movies Aunt Babe gave me, the next time I was home I surprised myself with an overwhelming desire to sneak back into Mom and Dad's bedroom to get another look at

Marlee's photo, the only vestige of the past I was aware existed in my mom's life. I now had my own copy of the photo hidden away, but something pulled me to connect with the one I'd seen so many years before.

I slid open the drawer quietly just like I watched Mom do on the day she revealed her secret hiding place to me. The smell of lavender wafted into the room and transported me back to that moment. What had I learned since then? My birth certificate had been altered to reflect my adoption. The photos from Aunt Babe convinced me of how well the family of Mom, Bob, and Marlee belonged together and how out of place my brother and I would have looked with them. But that was about it. I was a sorry excuse for an investigator.

I slid my hands underneath her sweaters. Instead of encountering the single photo I'd expected, I felt a stack of papers. I carefully slipped the pages from the bottom of the drawer and immediately recognized Mom's handwriting on the lined sheets of three-hole punched notebook paper. Paperclipped to the top of her pages was a letter with the words *Reader's Digest* stamped across the top. My heart skipped a beat. Why would Mom have a letter from *Reader's Digest*? It didn't take long to find my answer. "Thank you for submitting your moving story," it read. "Unfortunately, we are unable to publish it at this time."

Reader's Digest? Mom submitted a story to *Reader's Digest*?

I felt as if some invisible force pushed on my chest and forced the air from my lungs. This made no sense. Mom wasn't a writer. She'd never been a writer. Writing was so out of character for her that I might as well have discovered she'd come here from another planet. I sucked in a breath. And then another. And as I did, I sat down on the bed and began to read Mom's words.

"My daughter died when she was just eleven."

It's about Marlee. Mom wrote a story about Marlee. I stared at the text in my mother's halting handwriting, and her grief washed over me— a grief she'd already carried with her for over twenty-five years. And then, just as suddenly, the grief twisted into guilt. If I'd been a better daughter, couldn't I have assuaged her anguish, couldn't I have done something to make it better?

I don't remember what else she wrote. Today, I would give anything to recall more of her words, to know which memories she felt important enough to write about, which details she included, and to learn something about how she felt during that horrific tragedy. I remember thinking that the writing wasn't very good, that I could understand why *Reader's Digest* had rejected it. But on that day, I was too astonished to learn that Mom had written a story—written anything—about her life, to take in her words. I was too overwhelmed with my own insecurity about who I should be to her to focus on the content of what she wrote.

As I sat on the edge of the bed, I realized how much of my mother I didn't know, how much she kept hidden away, and how much I was following her lead. That's what stayed with me—the feelings we never shared, even more than the stories I never knew.

The book of Mom's life, and, by association, Marlee's, stayed closed to me. I didn't ask Mom about the story she'd written and, of course, she never brought it up to me. Her secrets had secrets, and she was so afraid of being criticized for the things she'd done wrong, she couldn't even share the things she'd done right.

I, too, was afraid—afraid of the answers Mom might give to my questions and afraid of the questions she might ask me in return. After I'd been exposed for having a "unsavory relationship," I spent most of my college days attempting to recover the trust I'd lost with my mom, by covering up who I was becoming. I had my own adult life to figure out and truths (and lies) to live into. Despite my nagging questions, those priorities would consume me for the next few years.

CHAPTER TEN

Intervention

"Have you ever thought about having kids?" Rick held a forkful of lasagna in the air as if he might be aiming it toward a toddler in a highchair. A big guy with black hair and a contagious laugh, Rick lived in the apartment below Michelle and me. He taught drama at a nearby high school, and although not out at his school, he lived an active gay life, regularly traveling to visit the leather scene at gay bars in Detroit. No one had heard of HIV/AIDS in the late-70s (the first case wasn't reported in the U.S. until 1981), so Rick, like many gay men in this time, relished promiscuity and the freedom of anonymity in his sexual encounters. But he also loved his students, and I could imagine him being a good father.

I squirmed in my chair at his question as I imagined Mom sitting across the table from me. "I've thought about it," I replied, not looking up from my plate. "It sure would make my mom happy."

I always responded defensively when Mom asked me about having kids because I saw it as a challenge to my sexuality. I identified as a lesbian to myself and among friends and worked hard to better understand how my sexuality defined me, but the closet door was only slightly cracked, especially with my mom. She saw it as an immoral choice that I was making to hurt her or that God was using to punish her. I did everything I could to avoid discussing the topic with her.

Most of my friends were other closeted lesbians, many of whom were members (or lovers of members) of our college basketball team. We found a deep comradery with each other, even if we rarely talked about being lesbians. As a result, I struggled with what it meant to live into this truth about myself. I'd taken a psychology class on sexual deviance and earned an A on a paper I wrote defending the morality of homosexuality (yes, at a Catholic college) but still felt uncomfortable with the perceived judgment others had of me.

Complicating this already too complicated situation, Michelle and I still lived together, even though she devoted much of her emotional and sexual energy to men. I longed to have her focus her attention on me, but that was not her way. I raged with jealousy but, whenever she decided to gift me with her presence, I welcomed her back into my bed. My insecurities had insecurities.

And above all else, I wanted to do everything I could to please my mom, to make up for the disappointment I was to her. To make up for being a lesbian. And more than anything, my mom wanted grandkids.

Every time she brought it up, I made the same argument. "I don't get it. Jarrett's son is almost a year old now. And he has an adopted son, too. You already have grandkids."

"It's not the same when your son has a child as when your daughter does," she bemoaned. "A grandmother can get closer to her daughter's children. That's what I want." She looked down like she was praying and added, "Don't you want to have children? You're so good with them."

To Mom, having children meant I needed to marry a man, and for all practical purposes, she was right. At least I needed to have sex with a man. Although intrauterine insemination (IUI) had been around for heterosexual couples for centuries (maybe as early as the 1700s, and possibly even before), it didn't become professionally available to lesbians until five years after I graduated college when, in 1982, the Sperm Bank of California opened their doors and welcomed lesbians and single women. In 1976, the only unmarried lesbians who got pregnant did it themselves with a turkey-baster—if they could find a friendly donor—or resorted to the old-fashioned way.

"No, Mom, I don't," I said, hoping to let the conversation drop. That usually stopped her, but every time, guilt burrowed deeper into my psyche. I yearned to please her as strongly, maybe even more strongly, than I longed to be who I was.

"Would having kids make *you* happy?" Rick's question snapped me back to the present, as he finally guided the forkful of food into his mouth.

Mom had never asked that question, at least not in that way. "Yes, I think it would. It would make me happy to have kids." I'd never said it out loud before. I'm not sure I'd ever said it to myself before. I want to have kids.

Without pausing, Rick said, "Let's do it then," his smile so wide I thought his face might break.

It might have been the wine. It might have been the food. It might have been the fantasy of finally finding a way of pleasing my mother, but I said yes.

To protect his teaching career and whatever job I'd end up with, we decided that we'd get married, with the clear understanding that our sex life would—ironically, much like many right-wing heterosexual couples— be focused exclusively on procreation. Whatever other private lives we had would be completely up to us.

It seemed like a perfect solution to the situation we found ourselves in. We'd have a cover for our "deviant" lifestyles, we could have kids of our own, and I could give my mother the grandkids she longed for.

"Oh, Annette. That's wonderful!" Mom exclaimed when I told her I was engaged. As if she'd been freed from the iron lung her polio-stricken daughter Marlee had lived and died in, she could breathe again.

I didn't tell her the rest.

Despite my engagement, Michelle and I moved from the spacious apartment above Rick's to a smaller, upper room on the other side of town—a temporary place until I found a job and could pay for something better, or perhaps until Rick and I got married and moved in together. A knock on the door interrupted my unpacking. I stood up awkwardly, trying not to trip over the contents of a kitchen box sprawled out in front of me. I hadn't yet told anyone where we'd moved, so I figured it must be someone selling something. Who else would it be?

With a diamond engagement ring shimmering on my finger, I flung the door open. Five friends from my basketball team stood on the other side—all members of the secret society of lesbians at my school. Several had graduated the year before me. I hadn't seen them in a while.

"Wow! Come on in! I'm so happy to see you," I said with enthusiasm, attempting to cover my hesitation with a welcoming smile. Except for Leslie who'd lived with Michelle and me in our last apartment, these were not women who came to visit much, especially not as a group. Something was up.

"We've come to talk with you," Mary said, her voice monotone and direct. "Do you mind if we sit down?"

"No, of course. Please sit." We didn't have a lot of furniture, so I gestured to the sofa, side chair, and ottoman, but also to the floor. They took their places.

"What's up?" I asked, already feeling nervous about the purpose of their visit.

Leslie cleared her throat and began. "We want to talk about your engagement."

"Oh?" I said. This couldn't be good. Although I still didn't know a lot of the rules of being a lesbian, I knew enough to know that other lesbians wouldn't look fondly on my decision to marry a man, even, and maybe even especially, a gay man.

I eyed the ottoman but chose not to sit there. Memories of my conversation with Mom years before when she confronted me about being a "homosexual" came flooding back. I'd learned my lesson that perching on a spherical blob in the center of the room is not a strong place to defend oneself. Instead, I grabbed a wooden chair from the kitchen, straddling it with the backrest in front as a makeshift shield.

For the next hour, maybe longer, my friends did what can only be described as an intervention on me.

"Do you love him?"

"How can you marry someone you're not in love with?"

"What'll happen if you have children and they find out?"

"Aren't you still a lesbian?"

"What if you fall in love with a woman?"

"What will she think of your 'arrangement?'"

I stammered to answer, even though I don't think I succeeded in finishing a coherent sentence.

After the questioning died down, they lambasted my decision-making and left no doubt that, in their opinion, I was making a big mistake. I felt as if I was on the bridge of the Starship Enterprise. Klingons were attacking, and Captain Kirk had just given the order, "Shields up, Mr. Scott." I needed more protection. The chair's backrest was clearly failing me.

I don't remember how we left things. I don't remember saying goodbye. All I remember is closing the door and leaning against it as if pushing hard enough would hold back a torrent of tears. It didn't work.

I stumbled to the sofa, put my head in my hands, and let the tears flow. The words of my friends echoed in my mind as I grappled with the weight of my decision. In the days that followed, I knew I had to confront the truth. Even though I didn't appreciate how their loving act felt harsh and uncaring, I knew they were right. I didn't want to have children if it meant giving up who I was. I could feel my body relax at the thought of being free again. Of being me again.

I don't know if I made the decision that day or sometime later. But at some point, soon after my friends' intervention, I found myself sitting across a table from Rick at some other restaurant hearing him say, "I need you to give me the ring back."

That shocked me at first, but of course, it made sense. I slipped the ring off my finger, dropped it into his hand, stood up, and walked away.

It was over.

All that was left was telling my mom that I wouldn't be getting married, and even more disappointing to her, that I wouldn't be giving her grandkids anytime soon. If ever. I wasn't looking forward to that conversation.

CHAPTER ELEVEN

A New Life

When three friends who'd volunteered to help me move placed the last boxes into my new study, in a new apartment, in a new town, I couldn't wait to close the door behind them. I thanked them for carrying what seemed like endless boxes of books, a limited collection of kitchenware and other household goods, and a hodgepodge of furniture up two flights of stairs. I then ushered them out the door. I had done it. All my stuff—what there was of it—was together again in one place. And it was all mine. I smiled just at the sight of it.

I felt like I could breathe for the first time since my friends' intervention that ultimately ended my ill-advised engagement six months earlier. After Rick and I broke up, I focused on the one thing that promised a fresh start: a new job somewhere other than Adrian. And I found one. I was hired as the executive director of a mental health/substance abuse crisis center in a small town about an hour away from where I'd spent the last six tumultuous years of my life. At only 22, this felt like quite an accomplishment, and I was proud of it. Though what it meant for Michelle and me, neither of us knew.

Even during my engagement to Rick, Michelle and I continued to be on and off again, unable to let go of each other. With a new job in another town, we'd finally have a reason—an excuse—to stop living together.

"I won't be commuting to Albion," I informed her, with a confidence I didn't feel. "I'm gonna move there. Get my own apartment. I guess that means you'll probably need to get a new place too."

It felt like a betrayal and, at the same time, a much-needed reason to move on with my life. Even if I'd married Rick, Michelle and I could have continued the dance we'd been doing for decades. I didn't know if I was still in love with her, but I knew what we had wasn't working. I couldn't stand seeing her with one more guy, and I'm sure she couldn't stand the thought of me marrying someone else, even if it was a marriage of convenience.

"Makes sense," she replied, shrugging her shoulders. Her voice flat as a stagnant pond with only the tiniest ripple to reveal any signs of life.

"You can come visit if you want," I added, sounding less inviting than I intended.

With things left hanging between us, I rented an apartment and began the painstaking process of separating our stuff.

"Do you really want *all* the Barry Manilow albums?" I shouted to her in the other room.

"Yes," she shouted back.

"Can't I keep one of them?" I countered.

"OK, but not 'Tryin' to Get the Feeling.'" Every time she relented felt like another thread pulled from an old sweater.

Although we hadn't officially ended what we had, we knew things were changing between us. Only time would tell what our relationship would look like moving forward.

I moved over the extended Fourth of July holiday weekend. The synchronicity of celebrating Independence Day as I crammed boxes with my meager belongings and secured their contents with heavy-duty packing tape wasn't lost on me. On July 5th, I started my new job, eager to immerse myself in my new community.

Two days later Mom called to tell me Dad was in the hospital. "Your dad had a heart attack" she said. "He's in ICU. You better come."

I winced at the news. I knew I had to go. That wasn't a question. I loved him and wanted to be there. But the timing couldn't have been worse. How could I tell my new employer I needed time off to fly to Arkansas? The interim director had kindly agreed to stay on for a month to orient me to the organization and the community. This would seriously cut into our time together. But when I said to her, "I have to go. I hope you understand." She said she did.

"We'll have enough time when you get back," she assured me. I had to trust she meant it.

The first thing I noticed when I entered Dad's hospital room was how pale he looked. I want to say gaunt, but Dad was a big man, so that's not exactly right. Maybe vacant is a better word.

"Hello, Netty," he whispered when he saw me, a smile not quite forming on his lips.

He often called me "Netty," one of only two people who did (Michelle was the other), and I loved hearing it from him. I sniffed the air to catch a whiff of his signature Edgeworth pipe tobacco—a smell I associated with him more closely than his cologne or after-shave—but all I smelled was the antiseptic aroma of hospital.

"Hi, Dad. What's all this about?" I gestured to the mass of IVs and cables hanging off his body. "Heck of a way to get to stay in bed all day."

"Yeah, but they have so many things hooked up to me, I can't even hold a book." He moved his hands to show how the cables restricted him. "See?"

Dad was still a big reader—mostly in bed—and his love of science fiction didn't die when Jarrett moved out.

"I hear ya," I replied. "That's no fun! We gotta get you out of here!" I raised my arm, formed a fist, and pointed my thumb backward toward the door.

He cracked a weak smile even though it lacked the Irish glint that usually accompanied it. I smiled back.

As I sat by his bedside in the days that followed, I told Dad about my new job, my apartment, and the town. I didn't tell him about my love life or anything that might cause tension between us. Over the years, Dad and I rarely talked about my sexual ori-entation—in fact I can only remember one conversation when I told him I was going out with Michelle's brother. He told me that it was just a ploy to stay connected to Michelle, and he was right. Now certainly didn't seem the time to tell him I was finally single but still a lesbian. Nor did it seem the time to ask him whether he was my biological father. Maybe some would have taken advantage of the opportunity for a hospital confession, but with all that was going on, I wasn't sure I was ready to hear it.

Although I knew Dad loved me and I loved him, we rarely shared anything personal. Typically, we talked about the news—he was an avid news follower and taught me a lot of what I know about politics. We talked about sports. Well, maybe I should say Dad and Jarrett talked about sports, while Mom and I listened. He especially loved football and hockey and spent a lot of time at my brother's football practices and games, so they had lots to talk about. And we talked about travel—something he did a lot of and encouraged us to do. Every summer, he took me on a solo trip as a way to spend time together. I'll never forget a trip to Memphis when Dad took me to a rock concert.

We were sitting at breakfast in the hotel dining room with newspapers held up between us as we devoured the morning news along with our eggs and toast. "Dad!" I interrupted his reading. "There's a really cool concert tonight here in Memphis. Gary Puckett and the Union Gap!"

He slowly lowered the paper, looked me right in the eyes, and much to my surprise, asked, "Do you want to go?"

I about lost it. "Could we?" I'd never been to a big concert before so had no idea what to expect, but yes, I wanted to go.

That evening, Dad and I sat on folding metal chairs on the floor of a huge arena with thousands of young girls screaming their lungs out. Dad tolerated the two opening acts, Joe South, whose hit song, "Games People Play" would eventually win Song of the Year at the Grammy's, and Kenny Rogers and the First Edition, who had recently won fame with "Just Dropped in to See What Condition My Condition Was In." But when Gary Puckett stepped on stage and started singing "Lady Willpower," the crowd went wild. Within minutes, maybe seconds, Dad put his hand on my leg to get my attention. He motioned backwards and mouthed that he'd be in the lobby. "Too loud," he exclaimed and with that got up and left me there.

I loved the concert, and I loved that Dad took me, but most of all I loved that he trusted me enough to stay there by myself. At 14, that trust meant a lot to me. And I loved Dad for it.

I'd been in Rogers for a week, and Dad was still in ICU. No improvement but no decline either according to the nurses treating him. When I entered his room on the morning of the seventh day, I didn't waste any time, "Dad, I have to get back to work. I'm sorry." I hugged him goodbye, trying to push aside my gnawing worry. "I wish I could stay." I didn't know if this would be the last time I'd see him, but I hugged him as if it were and told him I loved him. It was the best I could do.

I sat in my rental car in the hospital parking lot and let a few tears fall, then took a deep breath and focused on getting home. That was my way. Push down my feelings and get on with it. I was anxious to return to work and settle into my new life. I prayed Dad would be OK.

After two good weeks in my new job, I returned to Adrian to help Michelle move into a small one-bedroom apartment. It was the least I could do, I thought. For what, I'm not sure. It had been a full day of packing and hauling, and despite the almost full moon, darkness had descended. We were both exhausted. I reached into the trunk of my car, hefted the last big box into my arms, and headed for the door, looking forward to the cold beer waiting for me on the other side. The next thing I knew I was sprawled on the ground, the box and its contents strewn across the lawn, and my left elbow caught underneath me. I screamed.

"Are you alright?" Michelle called out and then rushed over.

"Ouch," I cried as she tried to get me up. "I tripped over that damn cement block!" pointing with my head. "My elbow's really hurting. Ow. Ow" I cradled my left arm in my right hand and tried to get up without moving it. It didn't work.

"Let's get you inside," Michelle said. "Do you think it's broken?"

"Yes."

"Damn! We'd better go to the ER. Go sit in the car," she commanded. "Let me get everything else inside. I'll be right back." I could hear the resignation in her voice. This was certainly not how she wanted to spend her first night in her new home.

On the following Friday, a week after my fall, I'd had successful surgery to repair a shattered elbow but was still in the hospital.

The plan was to release me on Saturday, so I could finally get back to work, in a full arm cast, on Monday.

I talked with Dad on the phone the night before I was discharged—from my hospital bed to his. They'd finally moved him out of ICU to a regular room, so he had access to a phone. We joked about both being in the hospital.

"We're a mess," I said.

"Yeah," he replied, "We both gotta get out of here." I could imagine his hand gesture mimicking mine from my earlier hospital visit.

He sounded better—a little perkier—and I hung up feeling hopeful he'd be OK.

Sunday morning, less than twenty-four hours after I'd been released from the hospital, my brother called me at Michelle's. "Dad died this morning," he said. "He had another heart attack."

I collapsed into the chair, cradling my cast into my chest like it was a tiny infant. "Oh, no!"

When Michelle heard my cry, she rushed over and hugged me without having to ask what had happened. In that moment, the challenges of our relationship melted away, and I welcomed her comforting arms.

On Monday morning, instead of returning to my new job, I flew back to Arkansas, cast and all, to say my final goodbyes to the man who was my dad.

I arrived just in time to meet Mom and Jarrett at the funeral home. When the funeral director asked if I wanted to see his body, I said no. Mom didn't want an open casket, so this was the only opportunity I'd have. I don't know why I chose not to see him. I guess I followed Mom's lead. I wish I had though. I now know that seeing him one last time would have provided me with a sense of finality that a closed casket doesn't offer. Maybe if I'd seen him, I could have let go of my nagging questions about whether he was my real dad and let things be. Or maybe not.

But at his funeral, I didn't think much about whether he was my adopted father or my biological father. He was just, "Dad," and I loved him.

By the time I returned to work, I'd been there a little over two weeks of the planned month-long orientation time and now it was two weeks past that. I'm surprised they didn't fire me. The interim director couldn't stay any longer. She had her own life to get on with, so I was left to my own devices to figure out my new job. And my new life. Now without a father.

As I finally settled into my routine in Albion, I grew more determined to embrace my true self as a lesbian and as a competent professional. I still didn't know how to live into either of those things, but I felt driven to find out.

Within weeks after Dad's death, I traded my beloved 1973 Pontiac Ventura hatchback, the car my dad had given me at my high school graduation and bought a sportier 1977 Pontiac Sunbird Coupe. Although I loved my Ventura, the car I named Vincent for Vincent van Gogh because I liked the alliteration, and I loved Don McLean's song about him, it felt like letting go of it was part of moving on, establishing my own identity, creating my own life.

Though my parents' secrets remained buried, I knew that the journey to uncover them would have to wait. It was my time now, and I looked forward to whatever might lie ahead.

CHAPTER TWELVE

The Second Coming (Out)

I unlocked my apartment door, tossed my briefcase on the couch, and threw my coat on top of it. I'd worked all day, then had back-to-back meetings well into the evening. On the short drive home to my apartment, winter's chill sapped every bit of energy I had left. All I wanted to do was change into warm sweats and curl up on the couch to watch TV. I knew, though, that would have to wait. I promised myself I would call Mom tonight. I usually called Mom on Sunday afternoons but the previous Sunday I'd chickened out. To call her on a Thursday would raise her antennae. She'd know something was up. But I didn't want to wait. It was time to get this over with.

As I sat down at my kitchen table, a train whistle interrupted my thoughts. My apartment in Albion stood just a block away from the same train tracks Mom, Jarrett, and I had traveled years before on our way to Denver to become a family with Dad. I liked hearing the train whistle blow when it approached the intersection behind my building. It reminded me of Dad. I missed him and wished we had had more time to get to know each other as adults. Maybe he would have come to trust me with the truth about whether he was my father, and maybe I would have come to trust him with my truth.

Dad's death and the secrets we never shared is what made me finally decide I had to tell Mom the truth about who I was. Six years had passed since Sister Barbara told my mother about my "unsavory relationship with another girl." Since that time, I'd done everything I could, including getting engaged to a man, to cover up who I really was, at least to Mom. I wanted so badly to be back in her favor. Even after I told her the engagement was over, I obfuscated when any discussion of my personal life came up. But I grew tired of hiding the truth.

I'd grown up around so many secrets, so many things we didn't say to each other, so much I didn't know about the time before I was born—and about the time after. I wanted Mom to know who the daughter she had raised to adulthood had become. I wanted her to be proud of me, to know she'd a done a good job, and if that wasn't possible, to at least know the truth about my life.

On the table in front of me was a small tape recorder. I brought it out the previous Sunday when I first decided to make the call. I don't know why I had the urge to record the conversation. Something told me I should. So much of my history had been destroyed, intentionally erased to hide the truth. I wanted to do things differently -- to start preserving the truth, even if it might be painful.

I paced around the apartment, first to the kitchen, then to the bedroom, then back to the living room. What would I say? I hated this. I hated telling her something I knew would upset her. But I still knew I had to tell her, even if the news would make her feel like a failure, as I suspected it would. What she wanted most for me was to be ordinary, to fit in, so I wouldn't be hurt.

That was Mom's highest aspiration for me: to be ordinary. If I were ordinary, no one would talk about me, no one would judge me, no one would have any reason to be mean to me. To Mom, being different made you vulnerable, made you a target. Maybe I shouldn't tell her. Maybe she'd rather not know. And yet I knew if we were going to have any kind of relationship, she needed to know who I was.

I rubbed my palms together and then rubbed them on my pants to dry the sweat. My stomach already felt like stone. I exhaled, then forced in another deep breath. Sometimes I thought deep breathing was overrated, but this time it at least gave me the courage to pick up the phone. I had to do this, not for her, but for me. I dialed Mom's number, and at the same time, pressed Record.

"Hello?" Mom always answered the phone with a suspicious, questioning tone, like "who are you, and why are you calling me?"

"Hi, it's me," What now? Damn it! Why didn't I plan this better? Where was that courage now? After a few minutes of small talk, long enough that we had run out of things to say, I held my breath and dove in. "I want to talk to you about some things, about some decisions I've made."

Silence. I imagined her hand tightening around the receiver. She would know it wasn't good news. It never was. To Mom, news only came in two kinds: bad and worse.

"I've decided to leave Albion and move to Boston." I pressed the phone to my ear with my shoulder so I could fiddle with a pen.

I had to do something with my hands. I broke off the pocket clip. I dropped the pen and grabbed the receiver again.

"To where?" she asked as if she hadn't heard me. I suspected it was her turn to stall.

"To Boston."

I heard her exhale, then nothing. I waited for her to take in this piece of the news. It's not that I was in a hurry for her to respond because that would lead to the next piece of news, and then the next. I knew this slice would be hard enough. She liked coming to visit me in Michigan; it felt familiar to her, like coming home. She wouldn't like the idea that I was moving to some place she'd never been. Michigan was home to me now, too. I'd lived there seven years, almost as long as I'd lived in Arkansas, longer if I counted the first five in Michigan before we moved to Denver.

After what seemed like enough time to drive to Boston, she asked, "Why?"

What Mom didn't know was that this was the easy part; there was more to come. "Well, let me explain some other things first, OK?" This time, I didn't wait for her to answer.

"Over the past few months, I've been doing a lot of thinking about me, and who I am, and how happy I am–those kind of things. And in fact, I've even seen a counselor to help me sort through some things. I feel like I'm in a place now where I really like who I am. I feel really good about myself. But the one -- the thing that I've discovered is, um, that I've come to accept in myself, and I'm not ashamed to say is that," At this point, I paused, inhaled, prayed for more courage. I had to say it if I was ever going to live with integrity. "I am homosexual."

I said it just like that, with all the prefaces, the hemming and hawing, and the word "homosexual." I know that because I discovered the cassette tape in an old box of memorabilia several years after Mom died, almost thirty years after that night. When I picked up the tape, I wasn't sure what it was. The label said: "Conversation w/ Mom re: Boston, et al. 11/30/78." I stared at it for a minute before it all came back to me. I'd completely forgotten it existed.

It took a few days to scrounge up a cassette player to listen to the tape—not a common thing most people had lying around in the early 2000s. As soon as I heard my much younger voice say, "Hi. It's me," it instantly catapulted me back in time to that dark night sitting alone at my kitchen table in Albion. My palms started to sweat, my heart began to race, and I felt my mouth go dry.

I strained to hear Mom's voice on the tape. Given that I only recorded my side of the conversation, I could only make out some of her words and her tone and inflection as she spoke them. I'd give anything to hear her clearly—to hear her voice again, even if what she was saying cut to my core.

It was an interesting choice that I used the word "homosexual." Even in the late 1970s, I didn't use that word when I thought about myself. I called myself lesbian—not "a lesbian"—that felt like a slur someone would hurl at me. Without the article, it sounded more like something I could claim as intrinsic to me. "I'm French, Irish, German, and Lesbian."

I'd just spent a year in therapy, trying to claim other words for myself like "dyke," "butch," and "queer," to take the sting out of them when someone used them against me, and to claim their power when I used them for myself. I wasn't quite there yet. A lot of people, especially men, used "gay" to describe themselves. Today, "queer" has been reclaimed by the LGBT community. But back then, I'm sure I didn't want any misunderstanding. Mom might think I meant "happy" if I used "gay," and "different," if I used "queer." So, in this conversation, I chose to use an unambiguous word, "homosexual"—the word I'd heard her use years before when she flung it at me as an accusation.

Mom fell silent after I made my pronouncement. Then, "You are?" It was more resignation than question, but I answered anyway.

"Yeah, I am." I closed my eyes and braced for her reaction.

I hated that I couldn't see her. What is she thinking? Why isn't she saying anything? I wondered if those words hit her the same as hearing that Marlee had polio. She blamed herself for that–thought God must be punishing her. Was this really much different to her?

In this second silence, I continued with my admissions, "I'm going to Boston with an old friend I've fallen in love with. And we've decided we want to be together."

Chris, a friend I met while still in high school, had come to stay with me over the summer. She was in a graduate program at Harvard and wanted to get out of Boston for a few months between semesters. I'd invited her to stay with me in Albion.

About midway through her stay, Chris and I acknowledged something we'd never let ourselves admit before—we were in love. This wasn't a new feeling for either of us, but for years, neither of us had acted on our feelings. Now things were different. I'd finally ended things with Michelle, and Chris and I were both ready to start a new life together.

We agreed she would return to Boston for school in August. Then by the end of the year, I'd quit my job, pack up my things, and join her. After I got settled in and got a job, I would apply to graduate schools myself.

Mom ignored who I was going to Boston with and zeroed in on my giving up my job. "How can you be so confident you're going to get another job?" "What kind of job?" "What if you don't find anything?" "How will you live?"

It was like waiting for a flood. I knew those questions were the leaks around the edges of the dam. At some point, when she couldn't hold herself back anymore, the dam would explode, and a river of blame, guilt, and denial would come roaring out. It didn't take as long as I expected. "Are you like this because I wasn't a good enough mother?" she asked.

"You are a good mother," I countered, then realized it wouldn't matter. She would just come up with another reason. "There's not a why, Mom. There's not a why. It's not anybody's fault. It's not something that happened to me. It's just the way I am."

"You're not really like this. It's just something you've talked yourself into being."

"Mom. I know it's hard for you to understand, but I don't want you to feel guilty about it either."

"How can I not feel guilty?"

"'Because it's not your fault. I know that you're going to take on all kinds of guilt, all kinds of regret, but it's just not worth it."

"I might as well just go crawl in a hole."

"Mom!"

"I don't have anything left."

"You still have me."

"I won't be able to visit you anymore."

"Why won't you?"

"I can't..."

"Why can't you?"

"I just can't!" Her voice raised a decibel or two, but neither of us was shouting. We didn't do that. If you couldn't say it calmly, it shouldn't be said. Mom's voice was more forlorn than angry, "Why is God doing this to me?"

The conversation went on like that for almost an hour. I feared the cassette tape would run out and yet Mom's tape kept running: It's a sickness, it's wrong. It's God's punishment for her sins. It's her fault. It's because I wanted to hurt her. It's because I wanted to make my own rules. It's because she let me go away to that boarding school. It's because I don't care.

"I do, Mother, I care a lot." Addressing her as "Mother" instead of "Mom" helped distance myself from the pain I was feeling. "I wouldn't be telling you in the first place if I didn't care. I could have just shut you off completely, but it was important to me that you know because you're important to me. I love you very much." I paused and let that hang in the air.

I hoped she might say it back. When she didn't, I went on trying to make her understand, and perhaps, trying to make myself understand why I was telling her this.

"Certainly, this isn't easy for me to do either, because I know how much it hurts you. But it's important for me that you know who I am, and to know that I'm happy in who I am."

I asked her if I could help her understand, if I could send her something to read that would help.

She said no.

When there was nothing left to say, we said goodnight. I pressed Stop on the recorder, ejected the tape, got up from the table, and threw the tape into my desk drawer. As I closed the drawer, I took a breath and whispered to the empty room, "It is done." Although I hoped for a different reaction, I got what I expected, and now it was up to me to figure out what that meant going forward.

Some people say that homosexuality is a choice. Mom certainly thought so. She thought I could talk myself out of it—be normal—if I tried hard enough. I knew differently. My sexual orientation was not a choice. The choice I faced was whether I would spend my life in the closet, afraid to let anyone know who I really was or live my life in the open with integrity and confidence. I didn't know if I was capable of the latter, especially without Mom's support. I prayed I would find a way.

Who knew I would catch my first glimpse of the possibilities at, of all places, a wedding? And not just any wedding, the first same-sex wedding I ever attended.

CHAPTER THIRTEEN

Smoke and Mirrors

When friends invited Chris and me to their wedding, I didn't greet the invitation with enthusiasm. It was the summer of 1980, a year and a half after I'd called Mom to tell her I was "homosexual." I now used the term "lesbian" and was becoming more comfortable with "dyke" and "butch," although only when used by and with other lesbians. I'd settled into life in Boston with Chris, found a job, and started graduate school —just like we had planned—at least for the moment.

I didn't like weddings. When my elementary school classmates played wedding instead of cleaning the church like we were supposed to do on Friday afternoons, I steered clear, and not just because I didn't want to get caught—although that was a key motivator in those days. I hated the thought of wearing a wedding gown and being the focus of everyone's attention. And even more than that, I hated the thought of belonging to a man.

In college, I developed political reasons for hating weddings. I viewed marriage as selling out to the patriarchy. It was bad enough when straight feminists did it. For two lesbians to adopt this misogynistic model to define their relationship made me cringe. I didn't want to condone their collusion with heteronormativity by my complicity.

But Chris wanted to go.

"Come on," she implored. "We haven't had time to play in a while. This will be fun."

I wasn't convinced. I was, however, intrigued. To encourage people to come, Kathy invited guests to camp on her parents' spacious Long Island farm property. Her parents were hosting their wedding? I couldn't imagine parents who would host their lesbian daughter's wedding. Given my experience, parents who supported their daughter and her girlfriend's wedding were as unusual as lesbians with dogs (something common today but an anathema at that time, when, at least in my lesbian community, it was all about cats). If nothing else, I said yes out of curiosity. Little did I know the wedding would be a watershed event in my life.

Just as Chris and I finished packing our camping gear for the drive, the phone rang. On the other end was Sherry, a woman we'd met a few months earlier at a conference for gay and lesbian seminarians sponsored by Harvard Divinity School—the first of its kind anywhere in the country. Chris and I liked her immediately and wanted to reconnect with her, but we didn't expect to hear from her so soon.

"Are you available for dinner tonight?" Sherry asked. She explained that she was in town visiting a "friend" and hoped to get together.

"Oh, I'm sorry, we're not," Chris replied. She looked at me and waved her hand as if she were trying to get me to agree to something, but I didn't know and couldn't imagine where she was heading. "We're driving to Long Island to Kathy and Megan's wedding this weekend. You remember them from the conference, right?" Then, without missing a beat and without looking my way, she added, "Do you and your friend want to come along?"

My eyes widened. That's what she was trying to ask me with all her gesturing? I didn't mind the drive, but the thought of four women with camping gear crammed into my Pontiac Sunbird for five hours to attend a lesbian wedding, of all things, didn't strike me as the makings of a great weekend. However, as was often the case, Chris's gregariousness surpassed my introversion, and this was one of those times. We couldn't uninvite them just because I didn't want them to come—just because I didn't want to go.

Within an hour, Sherry and her "friend" Anne pulled up in front of the house, threw their gear into the trunk of my car, and jammed themselves into the back seat. Minutes later, we were on our way. I had to admire their spontaneity.

It didn't take long before I relaxed into the trip and let myself enjoy their company. Both Sherry and Anne were educated professionals who knew how to have a good time. We shared coming out and how-we-got-together stories, laughed at various examples of our impulsivity, including this one, and talked about difficult subjects like discrimination against lesbians and gay men in ministry and other professions. Anne disclosed how she had been fired from a job as a college administrator in West Virginia because they found out she was a lesbian. Sherry was fighting with the Methodist Church about her ordination for the same reason.

Chris, who also dreamed of being ordained to ministry, struggled with the Catholic Church not only because she was a lesbian but because she was a woman. I drove and kept quiet. I hadn't faced this kind of discrimination personally, and the conversation reminded me how important it was to keep my sexuality to myself in my professional life.

When we finally arrived at our friend's house in Long Island, we piled out of the car, took deep stretches, and hugged each other. As much as I didn't want to make this journey in the first place and certainly didn't want to share it with anyone else, I knew we had become fast friends and was grateful Chris had pushed me into it.

As the wedding ceremony began a couple hours later, guests crowded into every corner of the rambling old Long Island farmhouse. In the living room, a man and a woman shared an old, worn leather pilot's chair, while three young children hung on to its arms. A few people leaned against the built-in bookcases, while others, standing three deep behind the sofa, jockeyed for a good view. Some men, distinguished by gray hair and closely cropped beards, sported suits with ties. Younger men with longer, less-manicured hair and goatees, wore jeans and t-shirts.

A lesbian couple, outfitted in matching dress slacks, collared shirts, and Birkenstocks, held hands as they squeezed themselves between the kitchen door and china cabinet. A few children spilled from the kitchen into the living room and then scampered out the front door, oblivious to the crowd amassed in their play space. More guests peered down from the second-floor loft. Laughter, rising and falling from the many conversations, infused the atmosphere with a joyful sound.

I don't remember what the two brides wore. I don't remember what the minister said. What I do remember is one minute feeling lifted and held, and the next, naked and exposed. A strange mix of possibility and panic rose up inside me. This was the first time I'd enjoyed the company of people, gay and straight, assembled for the purpose of honoring a lesbian relationship. Moms, dads, siblings, cousins, even a former Sunday school teacher joined in the ceremony.

I'd never imagined a world where lesbians could lead lives out of the shadows. Although I'd read about lesbians who lived openly, I didn't know any of them. Even the brides, Kathy and Megan, both students in a conservative seminary, lived in the closet back in Boston. I had no models to look to—no experience with which to trust what I saw. I tried to believe in the sincerity of the people in that room, but my mother's voice saying, "Don't stand out. Don't be different," drowned out the singing and obliterated the smiles. As an act of will, I purposefully tried to squash her words like an army of ants heading for the wedding feast. I yearned to savor every bite of this new world. And I was scared to death of it.

Somewhere in the middle of the ceremony, a thought wormed its way into my brain. It snuck up quietly. I didn't see it coming. If I ever had a wedding, I'd want one like this. Even the awareness made me grab onto a nearby chair to steady myself. If I ever had a wedding? What a ridiculous notion. I hate weddings, remember? Even when I was engaged to Rick, I never gave our wedding a passing thought.

For the first time, I wondered if I hated weddings because my imagination had never been big enough to encompass one where people would honor my relationship with another woman like they did Kathy and Megan's, where family and friends would embrace my joy rather than recoil from it. I shook my head to dislodge the idea from my consciousness. I'd held my distaste for weddings for too long to let it evaporate in a single afternoon.

As soon as the service ended, I fought my way to the door. I needed to breathe. When fresh air filled my lungs, the turmoil in my brain dissolved and I knew something had shifted. I had witnessed a new way to be in the world.

After the festivities ended, the overnight guests crowded around a campfire. As the effects of the alcohol and the darkness of the night sky relaxed me, the flames of the fire lit up the faces sitting around it. People exchanged stories; one woman strummed a guitar; a few passed around a joint; others sat quietly gazing into the fire. Couples huddled close to each other, women with women, women with men, and men with men—and no one minded. If only real life could be like this.

Up until that day, being a lesbian had felt like living in limbo, a place where my sexual identity kept me trapped in a world that was neither heaven nor hell. When I first identified as a lesbian, my life split into two uneven parts, a large public realm that held my school and professional life and anywhere it didn't feel safe to be out, which was almost everywhere, and a much smaller private world of my lesbian and a few gay friends. My family was somewhere in between—my sexual identity pervaded our relationship, but no one wanted me to talk about it.

I'd been fortunate enough to never experience the hell that some of my lesbian and gay sisters and brothers lived and died in. Despite my mom's painful response to my coming out, she hadn't thrown me out of the house, I'd never been fired from a job, and my professional aspirations hadn't been blocked.

At the same time, I didn't feel free to be fully who I was, to let people know me, to speak out for what I believed in. Sitting around the fire with this group of mostly strangers, I finally had an image of what it would be like if the gates of limbo flew open. I imagined the two parts of me reuniting into one being who lived and loved openly, an integrated whole. This new being hovered over me for a minute and then evaporated, drifting up and away with the smoke from the fire. The vision disappeared as fast as it had come. Still, I had a feeling I wouldn't forget it. I didn't know how to make it manifest again, but I couldn't deny I'd seen the possibility of a different reality.

As the night wore on, and the fire burned down, I surprised myself with the realization that I was having a good time. I noticed I was even glad Sherry and Anne had come with us—I enjoyed their company. I especially noticed the way the flames danced in Anne's eyes when she laughed. And I noticed that for those brief hours, I wasn't living inside a secret.

On the ride home from the wedding, I caught myself watching Anne through the rearview mirror. I didn't let myself think about the fact that I was already in a relationship or that Anne was, too. Caught up in the freedom I experienced from the weekend, I just let myself feel. By the time we arrived home, I knew I was smitten. Apparently, I'd find out later, so was Anne.

Over the next few months, Anne and I fell in love. That period deserves a book of its own—or at least a chapter in a book about relationships. But it's not the story I'm telling here, so I'll leave it with this: in what seemed like no time at all and, at the same time, forever, I ended my relationship with Chris, Anne ended hers with Sherry, and Anne and I decided to make a life together (not necessarily in that order). I quickly learned, however, that Anne's experiences of life in limbo would impact us in ways we couldn't yet understand.

Chapter Fourteen

Straightening Up

As soon as I heard Anne's voice on the phone, I knew something was wrong. Afraid that she'd been in an accident or something, I didn't hesitate, "Hon, what's up?"

The phone line fell silent and then, "They fired me." Her voice was devoid of expression—no affect, only words.

"What!?" I couldn't make sense of what she was saying. I must have misheard her.

"They fired me," she repeated it in the same hollow tone. "The dean called me into her office and said, 'we're letting you go.'"

"Why? What for?" I shouted—my throat tightened. Just the week before, she'd brought home a stunning performance appraisal. We'd gone out to dinner to celebrate. Even shared a bottle of champagne. As my legs started to shake, I sat down.

"She said 'I, I didn't,'" Anne gasped like she couldn't get air. "'represent the moral standards of the school.'" I could hear the emotion now. Anne didn't cry often, and I could tell from her wavering voice that it was taking everything she had to fight off tears.

"What!? Are you kidding me? That's absurd!"

"I think Laura must have said something," she whispered as if someone might be listening. Maybe they were.

Anne worked as the Director of Residential Life at a prestigious women's college in Massachusetts. It was her dream job—counseling and mentoring women in an academic setting. A few years earlier, another college in West Virginia found out she was a lesbian, or at least suspected she was, and dashed her burgeoning career in academia. She fought her way back from that abrupt termination to a better position at a highly ranked school close to her parents and her beloved family home in Maine.

But it hadn't been an easy recovery. After she was fired, she lived with a friend in Pennsylvania for a couple of years, taking odd jobs where she could. When she finally built up her courage to apply for another professional position, she did it at her friend's encouragement. She harbored no hope of being hired. When a school, and not any school—the top school on her list—said yes, everything fell into place.

She moved into a lovely old house on a tree-lined campus where she could walk to her office and then return home to her cherished rescue cat named Skipper. She hosted gatherings with students and staff where she could indulge her love of cooking, and during the summers, she joined her parents aboard their sailboat to cruise the Maine coastline. It was her ideal life, and she couldn't have been happier.

When we fell in love, she described it as the proverbial frosting on the cake. She was living the life she fantasized about. She really did have everything. The devastation she felt from her earlier firing became a distant memory—not eradicated, but also not something that controlled her. She was on a new course with a gentle wind filling her sails.

After we made the decision to end our other relationships and be together, our plans crystallized. I would finish my master's at the end of the school year and get a job nearby. In the meantime, we'd move in together—even though that meant leaving her precious on-campus house—and we'd live happily ever after.

To her, hearing her dean cast aspersions on her moral character because of our love felt like the mainsail had been ripped from the mast during a violent storm. She was instantly unmoored.

I sat in silence with her for a couple minutes at the other end of the receiver not knowing what to say, then finally asked, "Are you coming home?"

"Yeah," she answered without hesitation, "but I need to make a stop first."

OK, I'll see you when you get here." I had no idea where she was planning to stop and didn't ask. I was grateful for a few more minutes alone to prepare myself for whatever might come. Fortunately, I didn't have anywhere to be that evening. I'd been looking forward to a night off. Not anymore. My stomach felt like it did when we were sailing with her parents and the waves started bouncing us around like we were plastic bottles thrown out to sea. I needed time to collect myself before Anne got home.

When I finally greeted her at the door, I positioned myself to hug her, but when I saw she was clutching two bottles of wine, I stepped aside and let her in. Her intent for the evening became instantly obvious. She pushed past me, put the bottles on the counter, grabbed a glass, popped the corks on both bottles, and poured herself a generous portion.

"Help yourself," she said, waving her hand toward the wine as she grabbed one of the open bottles and plopped down on the couch.

"I've worked so hard to get back into higher ed. Then they pull this shit." She slammed her fist down on her leg and took a long swallow from her wine glass. "Damn it! Those bastards!"

I sat down beside her and reached for her clutched hand.

"Why do you think it was Laura?" I asked. "I thought she was fine with us." Memories came flooding back. A few weeks before, Anne and I had gone to San Francisco with Laura, one of Anne's colleagues. Anne and Laura went to attend a professional conference, and I went along for the ride. Anne liked Laura and trusted her. She thought we could take the risk of letting her know about us. So, when we decided to share a hotel room to save costs, it was Laura who suggested that Anne and I take the queen bed.

"I'll have them bring up a cot for me. I'll be fine," she assured us. Maybe the cot wasn't so comfortable after all.

Anne took another swig of her wine and refilled her glass. "She proposed a reorganization plan today that eliminated my position and gave her a big, fat promotion," she said. "She threw me under the bus." With that, she let go of my hand and turned her body toward the door as if she imagined running out of her life—our life—and back to the fantasy that sustained her before me.

"Oh, hon! I'm so sorry." As I said the words, I knew they fell flat. Did she blame me? If I'd left her alone to live her dream, none of this would have happened. Sure, her cake wouldn't have had icing, but it still would have been a sweet, delicious cake, one she could have savored for the rest of her life.

As I sat next to her, but not with her, my guilt fed my shame. I shouldn't have gone to San Francisco with her. We shouldn't have told anyone. If I were stronger, or better—or SOMETHING—I could have protected her. My mother's voice screamed in my head, "Don't let anyone know who you are. Fit in, be normal." I knew I would never suit Mom's definition of normal, but I'd learned enough from her to know how to keep a secret. We had violated the first precept of how to stay safe by letting our secret out, letting Laura know the truth. Damn it! I knew better! At that moment, as Anne stumbled to the kitchen for the second bottle of wine, I made a commitment to myself that I would never let that happen again. It's the only way to stay safe.

Because the school announced Anne's departure as a casualty of a reorganization plan, despite the immoral example they claimed she set, they let her finish out the semester, as if that was some kind of gift to her. But the woman who dutifully reported to work each day was an empty shell of the woman they'd hired a few years before, the one I'd come to know and love. When she came home each night, she cursed their hypocrisy, their homophobia, and their ignorance, and then got up the next morning and reported to work again.

Any hope that the doors of limbo would open soon, and we could live in a world accepting of our love, shattered with Anne's termination. I dove into caretaker mode. I couldn't stand to see her hurting, so I had to figure out a way to help. Although I applied for jobs in Massachusetts to start after my graduation, my heart wasn't in it. I wanted out of this place that had caused her, and us, so much pain. I didn't know what Anne wanted—and neither did she.

I figured if we moved to Michigan, where I already had an established safety net of friends, she could re-invent herself professionally. I didn't know if she'd go for it and I was afraid to broach the subject.

A few months later, when I was offered a position as the director of a women's alcoholism program in Lowell, just north of Boston, she seemed genuinely happy for me, so I accepted it.

Then two days later, I received a call from an old friend and colleague in Michigan offering me a different position as a consultant, a position that could turn into permanent employment. It's what I wanted to do, even though the risks surrounding the job were a lot greater. I'd be back with my friends and out of this place. But would Anne give up New England, the place she'd fought so hard to get back to, for Michigan farm country, especially when she'd already lost so much? I didn't know.

When I finally ginned up the courage to ask, Anne replied without a second thought. "Yeah," she said, shrugging her shoulders as if she didn't care what we did. "Let's blow this popsicle stand." So, we did. Within a month, we'd packed up a U-Haul, drove out of New England, across New York, Pennsylvania, and Ohio, and into south central Michigan where we would make a new home and, hopefully, find a fresh start.

In our new life, secrecy became a ritual. We'd failed at it in Massachusetts and suffered the consequences. We would have to be more cautious. Could we? Could we keep our secret as well as Mom and Dad had kept theirs—a secret I still didn't know the truth about? Did I really want to live like they had lived? For now, I was going to have to try.

Before Anne's parents came to visit in our Michigan home, we "straightened" up the house. Anne moved everything on her bedside table to the room we had designated as a guest room. She switched out enough of her clothes to make it appear that she used that closet. We hid away envelopes with both our names on them, cards we'd given each other, books about lesbian life. I stuffed photo albums into my closet so they wouldn't find any incriminating photos of us kissing or hugging each other, or even worse, photos from the Michigan Womyn's Music Festival, an annual refuge where thousands of lesbians gathered each August in the Michigan woods—a place where we looked forward to being completely ourselves for one week of the year.

When her mother expressed concern about Anne having to give up her room to them, Anne had a quick retort, "Oh, we don't mind, Mom and Dad, you go ahead and take my room; Annette has generously offered to share hers with me while you're here." She winked at me behind her mother's back.

"Here's my bedroom," Anne said, as she moved out of her parents' way and let them peer into the room on the left side of the hallway. "And this one's Annette's," she said, pointing to the room on the right.

We played this "straightening up" charade when anyone other than our lesbian friends came to visit. And they all played it, too. We laughed and joked about it when we were together, but deep down, it ripped pieces out of my heart, like the way Mom must have felt when she threw away photographs of her life with her first husband and daughter because my dad, Norm, wanted her to. I would be anxious for days before anyone visited, always looking, evaluating, identifying anything in the house that might raise suspicions.

We even checked the TV listings for shows that might have gay content in the upcoming lineup. We wanted to avoid those if we sat down to watch TV together. Network television didn't have a plethora of gay content in the 1980s but inevitably, whenever our parents visited, some TV news show would report on the "militant homosexual rights movement," or "the rise of GRID," i.e., gay-related immune deficiency, sometimes referred to as the "gay plague," (and now understood as HIV/AIDS).

If we happened to be watching TV and something gay appeared, a force-field locked on to all of us. We sat there stoically, without anyone saying a word or even moving a muscle, praying to be delivered from it. When the force-field finally released us, someone would jump up and say, "How about some ice cream?" or "I'm really tired; I'm going to turn in," or "What should we plan for dinner tomorrow night?" Anything to distract from the truth.

"Dear," her mother asked a few days into their first visit, "why does Annette have that lovely photograph of Buck's Harbor on

the wall in her room? I would think you would want it in yours."
Buck's Harbor was the site of the family's house in Maine.

Anne stumbled for an answer, "Oh, um, I've told her so much
it, and she thought the photo was pretty, so I let her put it up.
We thought it looked nice on the wall in there." Anne glanced
at me with a whoops-we-missed-that-one look.

What she didn't tell her mother was that I'd already been to
Buck's Harbor—several times. It was during my first visit there
that Anne and I admitted we were in love with each other. The
photo was one I'd taken that weekend. I hadn't even considered
taking it down. Like Mom holding on to that one remaining
photo of her daughter Marlee, I realized how hard it was to hide
such a significant part of one's life.

I found myself angry that I had to and, at the same time,
began to wonder why I was hiding myself. Sure, society's level
of acceptance of our relationship bordered on nonexistent, but
why did I care so much? Was I replicating my parents' pattern
of secrecy because I was too afraid to face recrimination from
others? Because I yearned too much for approval?

After the house was ours again, I returned books and photo
albums to the bookshelf. As I did, I flashed back to that kid
standing in the country store, fingers sticky from rummaging
in the candy bins, when Aunt Babe swooped in and stole my
typical answer about my red hair out from under me. That had
been the first time I felt what had now become an all-too-famil-
iar feeling. I felt dirty, irredeemable, not because of who I was
but because of the lies I told to keep others from knowing me.
Was this the way I was going to live my life? What would it cost
me if I did?

As I placed *Sappho Was a Right On Woman*—the book that first taught me about what it meant to live my life as a lesbian—back on the shelf, I sighed. Things were back to normal again—until the next time.

CHAPTER FIFTEEN

Duck! Duck!

A fter her firing, Anne never tried to find a job in academia again. She knew she couldn't handle a third strike—a third assault on her professionalism, her integrity, and the career she loved. Instead, she spent her first year in Michigan collecting unemployment from her Massachusetts disaster. She sat for hours staring out the window at the snow blowing across the cornfields behind the house we rented, something she referred to as "living in the tundra"—a far cry from her beloved New England.

We picked this house because it was as far away as possible from the non-profit where I worked while still meeting my board's requirement of living in the county. We didn't want to run into board members or clients at the grocery store and have to explain why we were together. Living in the middle of nowhere lowered that risk.

Through the help of a friend of mine, Anne eventually got a job as an alcoholism educator/counselor in a nearby town. The job suited her. She was a good teacher and a caring clinician. But going back to work terrified her. Even though the woman who hired her was a lesbian, she never felt safe. Would they find out? Would she get fired again? Her fears kept her from falling in love with her job—there or anywhere. She had loved working with college students. Treating adults with alcoholism is not the same as inspiring young women to prepare for their future.

When I was offered a management job with a large healthcare system in Detroit, we agreed to move once more, this time to the Detroit suburbs. Living just a few miles from Plymouth, where Mom met Norm, the man who would become my father, offered a constant reminder of the questions I had about my family, but I was too consumed with my current life to spend much time thinking about the past.

Anne commuted to her job for a while, and then another closeted lesbian friend who served the hospital as my co-director offered her a job as a chemical dependency therapist, essentially the same work she was doing but for higher pay at a more prestigious treatment center closer to home. Anne snapped it up.

"Should we drive to work together?" Anne asked as she focused her attention on ironing a white Oxford shirt for her first day.

I rubbed the corner of a magazine between my thumb and index finger as the smell of the hot iron wafted in my direction. I'd been avoiding this conversation but knew we had to have it. "It sure would save on gas," I suggested, even though I knew the answer to her question was no.

"But probably not, eh?" She paused as the steam rose from her shirt. "We don't want anyone to get the wrong idea."

I laid the magazine down. "Well, you know, I go to different to meetings at different places around Detroit most days anyway, and I never know when I'll need my car."

She hung the freshly pressed shirt on a hanger and stared at it for a minute. I couldn't tell if she was admiring her work or avoiding looking at me. "Yeah, makes sense."

"We can follow each other though," I offered. I didn't mean it to sound like a consolation prize. I turned to look out the window. The fall air hung heavy. I could see trees stripped of their leaves standing naked against the cloudy sky. "It's just probably better if we don't walk in together."

I stood up from the bed and reached out to hug her. She hugged me back. I wasn't sure if she would. I knew she wasn't angry with me, but still.

"You're gonna do great," I said, trying to sound reassuring but knowing my words rang hollow.

"I hope so," she replied as she pulled away and positioned a wrinkled pair of blue slacks on the ironing board and sprayed steam on them.

We never told anyone at work we were in a relationship or even that we lived together. We were friends, and that's all we let anyone know. What our co-workers thought, what they suspected, what they knew, we didn't confirm or deny. "Don't Ask, Don't Tell" didn't become military policy until 1994, but Anne and I lived it every day at work. When we weren't working, we occasionally socialized with other lesbians but spent most of our time with each other.

"Let's take a drive," I suggested one Saturday morning. We loved exploring the back roads and hidden-away places in Southeastern Michigan. It was our favorite way to spend a weekend. We got in the car and drove. Long before the days of GPS, we didn't care if we got lost or if we traveled the same road a hundred times. The fun was in the adventure itself, the hunt for something that surprised us. Maybe it was a field of sunflowers in bloom, newborn calves searching for their mothers' teats, a restaurant we hadn't eaten at before, or a trail we hadn't hiked. This had been one of those days. Life in limbo was good again.

As we headed home after a full day, I looked over at the car traveling next to us on the expressway, and, to my dismay, noticed one of our co-workers sitting in the passenger seat. It was a woman neither of us liked very much, someone for whom a rumor was like one of those plastic sea monsters you put in water and watched it grow to 600% its original size. As soon as I saw her, my protective instincts kicked in, and I shouted to Anne, "Duck! Duck!"

I expected her to lower her head so the woman wouldn't see us together. Anne, however, interpreted my urgency in the spirit of the day we had spent. Not wanting to miss something important, she lifted her head, pressed her face against the window, and shouted back at me, "Where? Where?"

When I heard the wonder in Anne's voice and realized what she must have thought I meant, I laughed so hard that I whipped the car across two lanes and onto the exit ramp so I could pull over. I was laughing too hard to drive. I laughed at the ridiculousness

of the situation, I laughed at the beauty of Anne's child-like curiosity, and I laughed at the absurdity of our attempts to hide our
relationship.

"What? What's the matter?" Anne asked. "What are you laughing about?" She smiled back at me but had no idea what had
happened.

Before I could answer, I crossed that razor-thin line from laughter to tears. The old Smokey Robinson & The Miracles song,
"Tears of a Clown" popped into my head. I felt like a clown
covered up in make-up and smiles, playing a fool. My entire life
was a sham, a farce put on to protect myself from being found out.
An erasure of who I was.

When I finally spit out what had happened—that I hadn't seen
ducks but meant for her to duck—I said, "I can't do this anymore,
Anne. I can't keep living this double life, hiding who I am—who
we are. I love you and I want everyone to know it. We have to find
a way."

Sometimes it's the mundane that turns on the closet light and
illuminates the door handle. This incident, as silly as it was, had
pointed out to me the outrageousness of living a bifurcated, fab-
ricated life.

"I wish it could be different," she said. I looked over at her, her
head pressed against the window, looking so vulnerable and so
loving. I could see her concern in her wrinkled brow and intense
eyes, and I knew she meant it. Then she added, "But what would
we do if we both got fired?"

At that moment, I recognized, for the first time, how living
in limbo had wounded us differently. Her two terminations had
humiliated her, preventing her from wanting to take any more

risks. While I was living life in the shadows to keep Mom's fantasy of who she wanted me to be alive and to protect Anne, neither of those reasons were enough for me to justify living a lie anymore.

As I pulled the car back onto the road, I knew we were finished talking. Anne put her seat back and pretended to take a nap. I drove on in silence recalling the vision I'd had sitting around that campfire at our lesbian friends' wedding years earlier. If there was any possibility that world might one day become real, I knew I had to seize it. I didn't want to be like Mom who, even in her later years, never shared her life, her pain, or her truth with anyone.

By the time we pulled into our driveway and Anne put her seat back up, I'd made a decision—I wasn't going to be erased any longer. What I didn't know is how to make that happen.

The route I took to finding my voice was unexpected, life-changing, and devastating. Ever since I'd left the Catholic Church in Albion years before, I'd had no religious home and hadn't sought one out. Although I missed the community, the ritual, and the sense of belonging to something larger than myself, I held no illusions about ever returning to church. Churches had no place for me, so I had no use for them. That is until I discovered that the minister of a nearby Unitarian Universalist (UU) church was a lesbian.

"She's an out lesbian? Are you sure?" I asked incredulously when a friend told me about her. How could that be? I was used to a church where even being a woman meant you were relegated to second-class status. But a lesbian woman? Unbelievable. I shook my head and at the same time, felt a glimmer of hope for the world—for us. Maybe we should go there, I thought.

Pretty much everything I knew about Unitarian Universalism came from Anne's dad. He was a Unitarian minister, and Anne grew up as a PK (preacher's kid). We spent weeks sailing the Maine coast with her folks and Anne's Dad told countless stories about his life in ministry and about his faith. His stories intrigued me, but he never told us we'd be welcome there, so I never imagined we would be. Despite being raised in the church, Anne hadn't joined another congregation. I'd never thought to ask why.

"Anne, you'll never guess what I just heard." The words tumbled from my mouth so fast I wasn't sure she understood me, but I couldn't stop the news from spilling out. "The minister at the UU church is a lesbian. An out lesbian. Can you believe it?"

I contemplated sitting down on one of our barstools at the counter where she was chopping carrots, but quickly realized I was too excited to be that still.

"Hmmm. That's interesting," she said without looking up.

"Let's go check it out," I implored. "That would be so cool!"

She paused from her chopping but stared straight ahead—not at me—like she was trying to remember something. "I don't know," she said. "I don't think any other minister, lesbian or not, can live up to my father."

I could hear the skepticism in her voice as she scraped the carrots into a storage container and grabbed a bag of celery. When she turned her back to wash the celery, I knew the conversation was over. At least for now.

A few weeks later, I learned that this same church was hosting a coffee house on a Saturday night. Anne loved music, so I suggested we go. She said yes, even though I was sure she suspected what I was up to.

Her suspicions were well-founded and before long we were regularly attending church on Sunday mornings. Seeing a lesbian process through the sanctuary and up to the pulpit made my heart leap. Every time! And not only did this congregation have a lesbian minister, but they openly accepted us as a couple. We could be out! And of all places, at church!

I think Anne liked this part, too. Holding hands while we sat together in a pew, sharing our lives with straight and gay couples in the fellowship hall, and celebrating other lesbian and gay people in the congregation made us feel normal—something we rarely experienced in our life together.

What Anne didn't like was my growing involvement with the church. I volunteered for the membership committee, the worship team, and eventually, the board. I started spending most of my free time at the church in one capacity or another. Anne didn't complain, but I could tell that she'd rather I stayed home with her. The final straw came when I told her I was considering enrolling in seminary to become a UU minister.

Her eyes grew big, her eyebrows raised, and she shrieked at me, "I will NOT become my mother!" I hadn't seen her scream like this since those horrible days after she'd been fired. It took me aback. "I will NOT be a minister's wife!" And with that, she retreated down the hallway and slammed the door to the bedroom.

I had no idea of the intensity of her feelings about this, so it caught me completely off guard. I shook my head as if I'd just been slammed to the ground with a knock-out punch. "You'll still have your own career," I countered, shouting through the closed door. "You won't be like your mother! You'll never be like your mother!" Her silence told me all I needed to know.

In some ways that I can't explain even today, her reaction strengthened my resolve to enter seminary. The world needed out lesbian ministers, and I needed to hold on to a faith community that would affirm me and my love of a woman.

I proceeded with the application process despite Anne's objections. I even asked Anne's father, who had once served as president of this UU seminary, Meadville Lombard Theological School, for a recommendation, which he graciously provided.

To do what I needed to do, to claim who I was as a lesbian and stand up publicly for the things I believed in, ultimately meant I had to hurt Anne. The "Duck! Duck!" incident was the beginning of the end for us. My plan to enter seminary was the breaking point from which there was no return.

It took two years from that first coffeehouse at the church, but I finally told her that our relationship was over. I was leaving. The more involved I became in the church and in lesbian and gay activist circles, the further apart Anne and I grew. She wasn't ready to be out, and I could no longer stay in. We'd been together for thirteen years and loved each other deeply. Neither of us ever dreamed we wouldn't always be together and neither of us ever fully recovered from the breakup.

Maybe if I'd been more confident in myself, I would have been able to help her through her fears, but I couldn't. Given the secrecy I'd seen modeled in my childhood, and my own internal battles, I had enough trouble managing my own fears. I knew myself well enough to know that I would find a way to keep Anne in my life, but it would be at a distance so as to not cause her more pain than I already had.

When I told Mom that Anne and I had broken up, she was genuinely sad. She never asked what happened or how I was, but I knew she liked Anne and would miss spending time with her. One day after Anne and I had taken Mom to Toronto for a vacation, she said to me, "I don't understand how I can like Anne so much more than your brother's wife. That's a little strange, don't you think?" I didn't. But that defined Mom's struggle better than anything. A pull from somewhere deep inside her said that what I was engaged in was wrong, so she shouldn't affirm it in any way. And yet, she couldn't help loving Anne.

I didn't last in seminary. I stayed for only one semester. I was too restless at that point in my life and couldn't imagine spending the next four years in school, followed by clinical pastoral education, a year of internship, and then a review by a committee that might decide I wasn't ready to receive fellowship into the UU ministry. The mere thought of the journey overwhelmed me. I was ready to get on with my life, and for reasons I still don't understand, pursuing ministry felt like putting it on pause. I deeply admire the many people who stay committed to this course, but I wasn't one of them.

So, ironically, one of the primary things that caused our relationship to fall apart, my plan to become a minister, didn't happen. And even more ironically, Anne was so distraught by my leaving that she came out to her parents. I don't know how that went, but she stayed in relationship with them until their deaths, so I can only hope they came to accept her.

We were both finally out, but for that to happen, we had to break up—and now we each had to find our own ways to live life out in the open.

Part Three

Chapter Sixteen

Historical Markers

More than ten years after I left Anne and three years after Mom died, I received a phone call that broke open the closely guarded book of secrets in my family. My secrets were already a thing of the past. My closet didn't even have a door anymore. I'd flung it open so wide that it broke right off its hinges. When I interviewed for a new job in Northern Michigan in early 2001, I came out to my potential employer during the interview. I didn't want any questions, any suspicions, any doubt. They would hire me knowing I was a lesbian, or I wouldn't get the job. They hired me. So, I packed up my things and moved to Traverse City in Michigan's Northern Lower Peninsula. There I began working as the Executive Director of Third Level Crisis Center, a job not unlike the position I'd held so many years before in Albion, where I confirmed to Mom that, as much as she hoped I'd grow out of it, I was a "homosexual."

I hadn't given a lot of thought to my parents' secrets over these intervening years. With Mom gone and only one living relative of their generation left (an aunt who married my uncle after all this had happened, and thus, didn't know anything), I'd pretty much given up any hope of finding out the truth. Instead of letting it worry me, I just let it go and focused on my own life.

Or so I thought.

When the phone rang, I almost didn't pick it up. It was the dead of winter. The temperature had hovered around 6 degrees all day, and I was cuddled up next to the wood stove reading some novel that I don't remember. I didn't want to be disturbed. "Let it go to the answering machine," I said aloud to no one.

Despite that, for reasons I still don't understand, I threw the fleece blanket off, stood up, and went to the phone. Out of habit I guess, or maybe I'd had some sort of premonition that this call would be important.

"Hello," I said, wishing I still had a blanket around me. Whenever my dad answered the phone, he always said what sounded like, "Yellow." I thought of him. I still do when I pick up a phone call. I didn't have much time to think, though. The woman on the other end of the line barely gave me a chance to finish with, "Hello" before she dove into her questions, "Are you Helen Marquis's daughter?"

"Yeees." I answered warily. Was this a sales call? It caught my attention that she knew my mother's name. The next question made it clear this was no salesperson.

"Did you have a sister named Marlee who died of polio?"

OK, now this was getting weird. I replied but with suspicion in my voice, "Yes, Marlee was my sister." I thought I could hear an intake of breath at the other end of the line.

"I'm Marcia," the woman declared. "I was your sister's best friend."

I glanced outside at the frozen Northern Michigan landscape, snow piled high on the deck, the only tracks those of birds trying to gather sustenance from the many feeders in our yard. I must have been cooped up in this house too long. Was I hearing things? If it was the same Marcia I'd heard about from Mom, it had been at least forty-five years since our families had been in touch.

Marcia didn't give me much time to make sense of what she'd just said. Before I responded, she started in with the reason for her call.

She talked fast and tangentially, and I struggled to keep up—to get the gist of what she was saying. She said she had been trying to find me for the past three years. She said something about going to visit Marlee's grave and finding out that she didn't have a headstone. She said she wanted to buy her one, but the cemetery wouldn't let her. She said they told her it had to be a blood relative. So, she said, she started looking for me.

And finally, before pausing for a breath, she said, "I have something to give you and something to ask of you."

I sat down. I felt like a character in an Indiana Jones movie who'd just been invited to go on a quest—if I was brave enough to accept the mission. Something to give me and something to ask of me. Whatever was she talking about?

Before I could begin to process everything that she'd already told me, she recounted all she'd done to try to find me: writing the state for documents, tracking down and calling my cousins, going to the library to look me up in city directories (do they still even make those?). As she went on, my own thoughts drowned out her voice. Marlee didn't have a headstone? What would Marcia have to give me? What would she want of me? Why did she go to such lengths to find me?

As Marcia kept talking, I found myself calculating how old she must be. If she were the same age as Marlee, who was born in 1937, I figured she must be close to seventy. I knew Mom had mentioned Marcia—in those rare times when she talked about her past—and she'd also mentioned Marcia's parents. I didn't know what had happened that caused them to lose touch. I assumed it was part of Dad's insistence that Mom leave her past behind.

Then I heard Marcia say, "My husband and I live in Flint."

My mind snapped back to the present. She and her husband live in Flint? I'd moved to Flint after Anne and I broke up and lived there until I moved up north for this job. We'd lived only a few miles from each other for almost ten years and neither of us had any idea about the other. We could have been sitting right next to each other devouring coney dogs at Flint's landmark diner, Angelo's, and we'd never have known.

When Marcia asked if I'd like to come to dinner, I said, "Absolutely." They were the first words out of my mouth since I said, "Yes, Marlee was my sister," and that seemed like a long time ago. This was big. I could finally learn about Marlee from someone who knew her besides Mom. Her best friend. And who knows what else she might know about my family? Maybe I could finally make sense of it all.

We made plans for the following weekend. I'd come to her house for dinner, and she'd explain everything then. As I hung up the phone, I felt adrenaline drain from my body. I hadn't realized I'd been so tense. I returned to my comfy chair, wrapped the blanket back around me, and stared into the fire trying to figure out what this all meant.

This unsettled feeling stayed with me as the week dragged on. The unanswered questions, the mystery, the secrets spun around inside my brain. Even though they'd lived inside of me, I'd masked them for so long I wasn't sure that I really wanted to unearth them. What would it mean to have answers to the questions that I'd given up ever knowing, questions that had shaped my life? It's all I could think about as I drove the four and a half hours from my home Up North back to Flint.

The neighborhood of small, brick ranch-style homes was typical of the industrial boom and bust town of Flint, Michigan. A smattering of unkempt lawns, damaged mailboxes, and run-down cars deprived the neighborhood of a homey feel. Marcia's house, however, appeared well-tended, despite the cracks in the driveway and an open garage full of boxes.

I rang the bell and waited. The door opened. A large, gregarious, billowy woman enveloped me in her arms. Marcia greeted me like long-lost family, the smell of talcum powder and sweet perfume overpowering my senses.

"It's so good to see you. So good to see you," her voice cracked as she let go of me and worked to pull herself together, straightening her skirt with her hands.

I told her it was great to meet her. "My mother told me so much about you," I said as I stepped inside the house. I knew that was an exaggeration—Mom hadn't told me much about anyone from that time, including Marlee—but the fact that I'd heard Marcia's name from Mom enough to remember it demonstrated how important she must have been. In fact, sometime after Dad died, when Mom visited me in Michigan, we tried to find Marcia's parents only to discover they'd moved to Florida. Mom told me that they'd been her and Bob's best friends. That's all she said. And all I knew.

"I loved your sister so much. I sure missed her when she died." Marcia shut the door behind me and motioned for me to head through the small, cluttered dining area into the living room. "Come in here," she directed as she pointed to a worn red couch. "Sit down. Make yourself comfortable. I'll be right back. I want to show you what I have for you." She hurried off into what appeared to be the bedroom.

While she was gone, I looked around. The house was dark, the furniture tattered, the air close. "Well-lived in," a friend of mine would say.

Before I had a chance to take any more in, Marcia returned clutching a beat-up, brown manila envelope. "This is all the research I did to find you," she said, plopping her large frame on the couch next to me. "It's got birth certificates, death certificates, marriage licenses, phone numbers, addresses. You name it. A lot of your relatives are in here," she said as she shook the envelope. "I took what little information I knew and tried to find out enough to figure out where you were." She opened the envelope and started pulling out the papers inside.

She did all this to find me? Two minutes on Google would have done it. But she was clearly not a Googler.

"I finally found you through your cousin, Kathy. You know, Rick's daughter."

Uncle Rick was my mother's younger brother—someone Mom didn't like very much. Something had come between them, but like all the secrets in my family, I never knew what it was. I hadn't had contact with his kids for years, so I had no idea how Kathy had information about me.

I flipped through the papers and there I saw it. Concealed by pieces of notebook paper, like the paper Mom used when she wrote Marlee's story so many years before, was a photograph—the same one Mom had kept hidden, even when Dad had her throw away all the others. The one Aunt Babe gave me when I first saw photos of Bob, the man Mom told me was my father. The photograph of Marlee on a horse. I pulled it out and stared at it.

It instantly transported me back to Mom and Dad's bedroom. I could see Mom searching for the photo under her sweaters in her dresser. I remember how I felt when I first saw it, the questions that formed in my head, the anger I felt when I learned that Dad had made her get rid of the others. Was I any closer to unraveling the mystery my parents had worked so hard to conceal? The answer was clearly, "no."

Marcia interrupted my reverie when she saw what I was looking at. "Oh, yeah, there are a few pictures in there," she said. "I didn't know if you had those. You can have them if you want. I've got others." She sounded as if she were offering me some store coupons she didn't need. She had no idea how precious these photos were.

"Thank you," I whispered, still amazed by what I held in my hands. Yes, there was the photo of Marlee on a horse, but also others of her and Marcia, and of Marlee as a toddler. Photos I'd never seen before, even if the batch from Aunt Babe I'd received years earlier.

As I tried to imagine Marlee's early years depicted in these snapshots, Marcia launched into the reason she had searched for me. "You see, Frank and I—he'll be back in a few minutes—are selling the house and going RVing. You know what RVing is, right?" she asked.

"Of course, yes," I snuck in before she was off again.

"I'm sorting through everything in the house, and I found this bracelet." Out of a smaller envelope buried deep inside the one with the papers and the photographs, she handed me what appeared to be a silver charm bracelet.

But it wasn't a charm bracelet. Instead of charms, ten Catholic patron saint medals adorned the tiny, tarnished chain, and five more lay loose in the envelope. I recognized a few of the images: the Sacred Heart of Jesus, Mary's Assumption into heaven, St. Christopher carrying Jesus on his shoulder. Others were either too worn or unfamiliar to identify, but I knew each one represented a special prayer, a patron saint, a plea for intersession. I loved medals like these when I was a kid and often wore three or four of them on a long, silver chain under my clothes. I always felt closer to God when I wore that necklace.

"Your mother made it and gave it to me after Marlee died. You see, it's made up of all the medals that children gave to your mother to pin on Marlee's iron lung."

I felt the air escape my chest as the gravity of Marcia's words hit me. I imagined a ten-year old Marcia standing next to that terrifying, yet life-giving contraption. I could hear air pumping through the monstrous machine that encased her friend's tiny body. I saw my sister's black, curly hair and her weak smile as Mom pinned another medal to a cloth draping her mechanical chest —a medal delivered by some child whose parents wouldn't allow them to come in. I imagined my grief-stricken mother collecting the medals from the iron lung, picking them off the cloth one by one, after Marlee's body refused to take in another breath.

As each medal passed through my fingers, I felt like I was praying a rosary. These medals, each one especially chosen for Marlee, represented the hopes, fears, and convictions of the many people who were pulling for her to recover. My fingers loosened around the bracelet, cradling the pain that seemed to burn from the time-worn metal, yet unable to release that pain any more than I could relieve my mother's grief—or my own.

I rested it on the table in front of me, and as I did, words long erased from the book of my family's past reappeared on the page.

"When I found the bracelet," Marcia said, forcing me to refocus on what she was saying, "I wanted to take it out to Holy Sepulchre, you know the cemetery, and bury it at your sister's grave." She didn't wait for me to answer but went on to reiterate the story she'd told me on the phone. "That's when I started searching for you." Marcia's flurry of words swirled around my head as I tried to grasp what she was saying.

"They probably couldn't afford a headstone for her, with all the medical bills and everything," I offered.

I knew from the few stories I'd heard that Mom and Bob didn't have a lot of money after Marlee died. Michigan Bell, where Bob worked, was on strike, and he was so desperate for money he defied the picket lines and worked anyway. Already ostracized from the community for having a daughter with polio, becoming a scab isolated them even further.

But this oversight—not buying your daughter a headstone--if that's what it was, felt so unlike Mom. She would have wanted a headstone for her daughter. Wouldn't she? I couldn't imagine what would have prevented her from finding a way. Was it too painful to see Marlee's name carved into a block of stone? Was that their way of holding on to her? Or was it their way of letting go? Or, perhaps, this was another way to erase the past.

I assured Marcia I'd arrange for Marlee to get a headstone. "That's what you're asking, right? You want me to get a headstone for Marlee."

She nodded yes in an almost frantic way. "Her father, you know, Bob, doesn't have one either," she said. "I asked about that too."

"Really?" I noticed she said "her father" and not "your father." Maybe that was just because Marcia only knew him as Marlee's father or maybe...maybe she knew something I didn't. Learning that both of them rested in unmarked graves unnerved me, like the missing photographs. Their story, their lives, had been expunged as if they never existed.

Having a task to focus on helped bring me back from imagining what Mom and Bob went through after Marlee died. "I'm happy to make arrangements for them both. They deserve to have their lives marked."

We worked out a deal where I'd order a headstone and tell her how much it cost. Then, she'd send me $50 a month until she had paid off half of it. I told her she didn't have to do that, but she insisted.

"I want to do it," she said, tears welling up in her eyes. "She was my best friend." And with that, she hugged me again.

We sat there together in silence as if honoring a sacred trust. I thought about how Marcia had held onto Marlee all these years. I looked again at the girl on a horse in the photograph. She must have been a special child to create this deep loyalty from a childhood friend. I again wished I'd known her. She would have helped answer my questions, to understand what really happened before Uncle Norm became Dad. My parents had done such an effective job splitting our lives into before-Norm and after-Norm, I never imagined what my life would have been like if Marlee had lived. Would I have even had a life?

As I left Marcia's that evening, I clutched the envelope with the bracelet inside, just as she had done when she first brought it out to me. I hugged her for the third time. "Thanks for searching for me for so long," I said as I released her and turned toward my car. "I'm glad we finally found each other after all these years." And I meant it, despite, or maybe because of, the story she'd shared with me. I promised her I'd be back in touch, "just as soon as I find out about the headstones."

My parents, for reasons I didn't know, had tried to erase the past. Now I had an opportunity to reclaim a piece of it—to proclaim that Robert L. Smith and his daughter Marlee Lucille had lived and died. I still didn't know much about them. I didn't know if Bob was my father and Marlee my full sister as my parents had insisted, or if some other truth lay hidden in Marcia's stack of papers. All I knew was that they were both a part of my story. If I was ever to understand who I was and where I came from, I first had to claim them as my own.

CHAPTER SEVENTEEN

Do You Want to Know?

A few months after Marcia and I first met at her home and she asked me to purchase a headstone for my sister, Marlee—her dear friend—I visited Marcia again. This time I had something to give her instead of the other way around. I pulled out two photographs from my jacket pocket: one showed Marlee's headstone and the other, the stone for Marlee's father, Bob. I placed them on the table in front of her.

"Oh, they're beautiful," Marcia exclaimed. "Just what I imagined." I thought I could detect a tear rolling down her cheek, but she wiped it away with one hand while she picked up the photo of Marlee's headstone with the other. She pulled it to her chest and held it there, closed her eyes, and mouthed, "Thank you."

I wasn't sure if she was thanking me or God, but I stayed quiet while she took in this moment. It had been over three—almost four years—since she first learned that Marlee didn't have a headstone and set out on a quest to get her one. In this moment, she realized that she'd accomplished her goal—her quest fulfilled.

"Thank you," she repeated, but this time she looked at me, and I knew she was grateful I'd taken this on and gotten it done.

I'd kept the headstones simple, nothing fancy, flat granite stones with just their names, birth and death dates, and on Marlee's, the words "Our beautiful daughter", and on Bob's, "Beloved husband and father." But there's power in simplicity, and I could feel it rising from these two spirits who'd lived, loved, and died long before their time.

Although I still had many questions about them, with these headstones, their lives were no longer invisible, unmarked, unnamed. I felt good about that, like a long, unfinished chapter had finally been completed. At least couples strolling through the cemetery on a spring day, or a writer listening for stories in the words engraved on headstones, would see their names, would recognize they existed.

Marcia and I sat in her cramped kitchen, almost as if in prayer when her husband passed through and excused himself to go work in the yard. At that, she stood up and invited me to move to the living room.

"We'll be more comfortable in there," she said as she motioned toward the other room, "so we can talk some more."

I swallowed hard. Was this the time, at last, to talk with her about my parents—to try to finish another chapter? I didn't know if she knew anything, but she was the only person alive who might. Even if she did, would she tell me what she knew? I could feel anxiety rising in me. If I heard the truth, would it unleash the feelings I'd kept so carefully controlled all these years? What would

I do with the truth? How would it impact my life? I didn't know the answers, but I decided I had to give her the opportunity.

"I know our parents were good friends at one time," I ventured, meaning her mom and dad and my mom and Bob. "But something must have happened to make them lose track of each other. I never knew what it was." That was the best I could do. Not exactly a question, but I had a feeling it was somehow related. Would she pick it up from there?

Marcia looked at me as if she were trying to assess my stability. Her eyes narrowed, her brow furrowed, and she took a breath. "Do you want to know?" she asked, her voice soft, tentative.

For a split second, I tried to think of any scenario in which I might not want to know, but my mind betrayed me. It refused to think in full sentences. Instead, it filled with images. The haunting image of my sister Marlee, her small body encased in the iron lung that filled the living room of our family's home. I could almost hear the mechanical whoosh and sigh of the machine forcing air in and out of her lungs, could almost see the desperation etched on Marcia's face as she kept vigil by her friend's side. This image, though never witnessed firsthand, was seared into my mind, a ghostly specter of the pain endured by those who loved Marlee.

And other images flooded my mind: snapshots of Dad taking his pipe out of his mouth to wrap his arms around my brother and me when he greeted us at the Denver train station, my Aunt Babe appearing to cover up the source of my red hair to the clerk at the corner store, Mom almost crying the day she dug the photograph of Marlee on a horse out of her dresser drawer. I heard that Denver train whistle blow and felt the cool waters of the Arkansas crawdad creek I escaped to as a child wash over me. I could taste the velvety smooth chocolate frosting of Marquis Chocolate Cake—the cake I savored at Uncle Norm and Aunt Betty's restaurant—melting on my tongue, a cake that represented the warmth and love I felt in their presence so long ago.

Before I stopped myself, I heard myself saying, "Yes, of course. Sure."

"Ok, then," Marcia replied.

I steeled myself. This might be it.

Marcia looked at me. She began softly, her speech significantly more measured than in our previous conversations. "When my father was dying, he was pretty lucid for a long time and spent the time reviewing his life. He told me he was sad about some things over the years but was especially sad about losing his friendship with your mom and Bob."

So, I was right, something had come between them.

"When Marlee died," she went on, "Bob became so depressed that he couldn't function, and he and your mom separated for a while."

I knew the first part; the second was news. They separated? I tried to imagine how bad it must have been for Mom to decide to leave. My ears started ringing, and I had to lean forward to hear her.

"Your mother went to stay with her sister, your Aunt Babe." Marcia paused as if letting me absorb what she'd already told me or prepare for what was coming next. Mom stayed at Aunt Babe and Uncle Paul's farm? The house, a converted two-car garage, was barely big enough for the two of them. I couldn't imagine Mom, who required as much privacy as I did, being comfortable living there.

"It was during that time," she went on while images of the farm still flooded my brain, "that your mom got pregnant with Jarrett."

When Bob and Mom were separated? She became pregnant with Jarrett when they were separated? I felt a chill and looked around to see where a cold draft might be coming from. Not finding the source, I rubbed my arms to warm myself. It didn't work. That means Jarrett is definitely not Bob's son.

Marcia paused for me to absorb this revelation before she continued.

"Bob took her back because that's what decent men did then." Almost as an aside, she added, "But it didn't last very long. Your mom decided to get a divorce."

At that point, Marcia paused again. I assume to assess how I was receiving the information so far. Good call. I was close to hyperventilating but trying hard to appear calm. I didn't want to let my feelings get the better of me—especially not in front of a relative stranger.

Mom was planning to get a divorce? Processing the incongruity of that information about the devoted Catholic woman I knew made it hard to keep listening. It must have been bad. That was not something good Catholic women did in the 1950s and certainly not something my long-suffering mom would have done without a significant motive. Had Bob, in his grief, become violent? Had he mistreated her in some way? Did he blame her for Marlee's death? So much to think about.

Marcia's husband chose this moment to come into the house from outside. "Getting pretty dark out there," he said, as he passed through the living room and into the back of the house.

"Glad you came in then, Neil," she shouted toward him, even though he was now out of view.

This brief interruption gave me time to brace for what was coming next. I gripped the arm of the sofa, sat up a little straighter, and pushed my shoulders back.

Marcia resumed. "Your mom went to stay with Babe, again," and without pausing, added, "and again found herself pregnant."

That's the way Marcia said it, "found herself pregnant" as if Mom were the Virgin Mary and the Holy Spirit had descended upon her.

I was that child.

Marcia didn't give me much time to absorb this revelation before telling me that Bob took Mom back a second time, and that they had only been back together a couple of months when he suffered his fatal heart attack. I pictured him standing in the Sunday buffet line at Uncle Norm and Aunt Betty's restaurant when he collapsed.

"He died before the ambulance came," she added. I sensed her grief at losing her best friend's father—a man who welcomed her into their home when his daughter was dying of polio. I wondered what she thought of him.

Marcia hesitated before going on. She looked me in the eye and grabbed my hand to hold it in hers, as if she were about to tell me someone had died. When she could see she had my attention, she proceeded. "Norman is your real father, you know."

The room fell silent as the words on my adoption decree flashed before my eyes: "The petitioner (Norman W. Marquis) has good moral character... that the best interests of said child will be served by said adoption... that Robert Leo Smith, the natural father of said child is deceased." I'd read it so many times I could almost recite the whole thing. It was all a lie!

"Oh yeah, I know." My voice sounded loud, like we were in an echo chamber. I said it in the same nonchalant way I used to say my red hair came from my father. I said it as if I had always known. I said it as if it was no big deal. I said it as if it was confirmation of something I'd been told before instead of an answer to a question that I'd harbored since I was a child, since that day in the store with Aunt Babe.

I did know—deep down inside I knew—but hearing her tell me the story, hearing her say the words etched them on my heart in a way I'd not experienced before, made them permanent like the words engraved on Marlee's and Bob's headstones.

I folded my arms in front of me and squeezed, but I couldn't protect myself from the pain. I should be relieved that I finally had my suspicions confirmed. But the relief didn't come. And still, I did what my mother had taught me so well—I showed no emotion. I didn't let on how her story had affected me. Even with this secret blown open, I would keep my feelings locked away in a closet not unlike the one I'd broken free of so many years before.

"My father," Marcia said, "couldn't forgive your mother for having children outside of her marriage. It went against everything he believed in. But when he was dying, he regretted cutting her off. He wished he could have stayed in her life, that he would have allowed me to stay in her life. He felt bad that he left her alone to grieve Bob's death."

I don't remember how I responded to this revelation, except to say that I was sorry they'd lost touch.

When I left Marcia's house, I thanked her for telling me the truth and for being there for Marlee. I left the photographs of the two headstones—marking the lives of two people whose untimely deaths set off a complicated chain of events I was only beginning to grapple with.

The next day, I couldn't remember how I got home from Marcia's house, the route I took, the traffic I encountered. Everything from the evening blurred like a film out of focus. Except, that is, for the apprehensive look on Marcia's face—her brow furrowed, forehead creased, and eyes filled with compassion and concern—when she said the words, "Norman is your real father, you know." I'm sure she didn't know what to expect when she revealed this news: what I knew, what I didn't, and how I might react.

For the next few days, I wandered around the house, unable to concentrate, willing myself not to feel—and failing. Like a call and response at a Southern revival, Marcia's assertion reverberated in my head, "Norman is your real father, you know," and Mom's invitation from so long ago, echoed in response, "You can call him Dad."

Norman is your real father, you know. You can call him Dad.

Norman is your real father, you know. You can call him Dad.

I ruminated on the questions I carried for so long: why did Mom and Bob wait sixteen years after Marlee's birth to have another child? Why were Jarrett and I born so close together (21 months) after that gap? Why did Dad make Mom sever all her ties with her past? Where did my red hair come from?

Marcia's story resolved all those questions. But even as the fog on the window to the past cleared, I didn't want to look through it for fear of what I might see on the other side.

For months after, I resisted letting the truth of Marcia's words settle inside me. I knew if I did, if I accepted her father's version of the story, I would have to accept that these two devout Catholics not only violated the Church's teachings about divorce but had a multi-year affair that produced two illegitimate children—and I was one of them. I would have to acknowledge that my parents conspired to fabricate and maintain a complicated tale to protect my brother and me from knowing our spurious roots, safeguard their own reputations, and, most painfully, shield us from a truth they erroneously believed would harm us.

My anger rose like a wall, keeping the truth at bay—a simmering fury about how their shame had erased the truth of my life.

If I let that wall fall, I would have to accept that they allowed me to grieve for a dead father when my real one was right in front of me.

All those years when Dad was still alive and I knew him only as my godfather, my stepfather, and finally, my adopted father, felt stolen from me. The secret had destroyed the opportunity to love my dad as my own biological father.

If I let that wall fall, I would have to admit how much of my life was a lie.

CHAPTER EIGHTEEN

Revisionist History

I let some time pass—a few days, a few weeks, I don't remember—and then finally screwed up my courage to call Jarrett and tell him the story Marcia had related to me. I knew telling him was giving her story legitimacy, even if I expressed any lingering doubts I could still muster.

I related the story of how Marcia found me, what she told me about Marlee, and about the headstones, the bracelet, and the photos, and then I said the words, "Marcia said her dad told her Norman was our real father." I let the declaration hang unsupported in the air between cell towers. Before it crashed to the ground with the weight of the silence, I swooped in to the rescue, "What do you think?"

Jarrett's stoicism could win awards, so I didn't expect much response, but I wanted to hear something. He surprised me when he said, "Before she died, I asked Mom if Norm was our real dad. She denied it." He paused and then added, "But I think he was."

The chant that resounded unabated in my head made room for another verse:

Norman is your real father, you know.

She denied it, but I think he was.

You can call him Dad.

"Yeah, you're probably right," I finally said. I longed to say more. I wanted to tell him how angry I was they never told us, how sad it made me to think of what they went through to hide it, how hurt I was that they could never trust us enough. But that's not what we do. "I guess there's no way to know for sure," I said, "now that they're both dead."

That was the extent of our conversation.

A few days later, I received an email that suggested Jarrett had been ruminating as I had. The subject line, "Origin Theories," sounded like the detached scientist he liked to pretend he was, but I knew him well enough to know the news I'd shared had troubled him, too. I opened the email with a small amount of trepidation—I wasn't sure I was ready for more.

The email simply said, "Here's Carolyn's theory." Carolyn was Mom's best friend and someone who held Mom in the highest regard. I felt that deep-rooted, genetic fear of what people would think rise inside me. *I wish he hadn't shared it with Carolyn.* I hated to think Carolyn's opinion of Mom might change. Then I caught myself. I was at it again—operating from my old secret-keeping, protectionist place I'd worked so hard to move on from. That's what got us into this mess to begin with, being so concerned with what others would think that our parents erased the truth of our lives as if it were graffiti on a bathroom wall. I knew nothing could impact Carolyn's love for Mom, and she might have some insight that could help us understand this whole thing.

Carolyn knew Mom better than anybody. If she had a theory that was different than Marcia's, I wanted to know it. I had to know it. Perhaps she had figured it out, maybe she knew something she had never disclosed, maybe her version might get me closer to the truth—or at least help me understand it.

I clicked to open the email and instead of a story, I saw two lists. One labeled "Facts" and the other, "Theory." I assumed the facts had already been established, so I didn't expect any surprises there.

Facts

- *Helen and Norm were both devout Catholics, as I suppose were Bob and Betty.*

- *Helen always put others before herself.*

- *Helen would do anything for the ones she loved.*

- *Helen was always very conscious of what others thought.*

- *I always knew there was something "big" bothering her but could not press her to tell me.*

- *Helen and Bob and Norm and Betty were very close friends who spent time together.*

- *Helen loved Bob very much, from all I heard her say.*

- *Bob never got over the loss of Marlee.*

- *Bob and Helen were married a number of years before Marlee was born.*

- *Marlee was 11 years old when she died and they never had any other children.*

Two of Carolyn's "facts" caught my attention. Carolyn and Mom became closest after Mom discovered I was a lesbian. It's possible that the "something big that was bothering her" was not related to our origins but instead to my sexual orientation. When I came out to Carolyn after Mom had died, she said, "I've known that since you were in high school, and its fine with me, but I never wanted to bring it up to your mother. I figured if she thought I didn't know, she would believe her secret was safe."

So, the "something big" Mom hid so well from her best friend could have been our origins, could have been my sexual orientation, or could have been a combination of the two. If Mom had only trusted that Carolyn would love her no matter what, perhaps she could have found a way to tell us the truth, and maybe even come to accept me. I wished Carolyn had found a way to break the lock on Mom's lockbox. It could have made a big difference.

I also found it curious that one of Carolyn's "facts" clearly states that, "...they [meaning Mom and Bob] never had any other children." That indicates Carolyn is certain we are not Bob's children. How did she establish this as a "fact," I wondered?

I read through the facts a second time before moving on to *Theory*. I wanted to make sure I hadn't missed anything, and truthfully, I wanted to stall before being forced to consider another possibility.

Theory

- *Helen would do anything to help Bob with his deep depression.*

- *Helen wanted to have another daughter for Bob to love.*

- *They were unable to have more children for whatever reason.*

- *Norm volunteered to "help" and so Helen had a son, not a daughter.*

- *It did not help Bob's depression.*

- *Norm again offered to help and this time it was a girl, but Bob had died and never knew.*

- *Did Bob die of a heart attack from finding out the truth? Or just from "giving up"?*

- *Daisy moved to Rogers, Norm's restaurant closed and he went to work for Daisy in Denver.*

- *Norm asked Helen to marry him so he could help raise "his" children.*

- *He also cared a great deal for Helen, as well.*

- *Helen agreed and moved to Denver where they were married.*

Whoa! That's quite the theory. And so strange to see it as a bulleted list, I thought, as if a fuller presentation to elucidate each point was waiting to be told, a defense attorney preparing to make her closing statement. Her concluding paragraph summed it up.

"I am sure you have thought of all sorts of things, and like you, I could believe part of the story but not the rest. Helen could NEVER just have an affair. I would stake my life on it. There has to be more to the story."

In a subsequent email, Carolyn questioned Marcia's and her parents' credibility. I figured that came from Carolyn's own struggle to accept that Mom and Dad, especially her dear friend, Helen, could do something that inconceivable. Carolyn adored my mom so much that she couldn't ever think of her as a sinner. Instead, she created this alternate scenario that ascribed honorable motivations to Mom's behavior. I couldn't blame her for that.

And, who knows, maybe she was right. I needed that, too. If I accepted the fact that Norm was my father, something that was becoming harder to deny, I wanted to learn that Mom and Dad did not intentionally set out to hurt Bob and Betty, or to hurt Jarrett and me. I longed to discover there was something more to the story, something that explained why it was so difficult for them to share the truth.

It was time to dust off my detective skills and do a systematic review of what I knew, some of which I'd gleaned from Mom over the years, a little I learned from Dad, some from Marcia over our visits and phone calls -- and some from my own scrutiny of records, census data, and other sources. Maybe, somewhere in there, I could understand why they did what they did, how it happened, and why they worked so hard to cover it up. It was my hope that in understanding this, I could answer my real question, how did the secret, kept or told, make me who I am?

CHAPTER NINETEEN

All the Truth I Thought I Could Know

S craps of paper, official government documents, old photographs, newspaper articles, audio and video tapes, and letters littered my desk and the floor around it. Each document, each
story I'd heard at some point over the years held some piece of the
truth, of someone's truth. As I sat in a chair in my study, I picked
up each artifact, one by one, and listened carefully to the story
it held. Mom had already been dead eight years, Norm almost
thirty-five. Anything I could know, I already did. All I could do
now was try to make sense of it.

My journey toward understanding the motives that drove my
parents to erase the time before my birth had to begin with what
I knew about Mom's life.

Mom was born in 1913 in Detroit, Michigan, as Helen Mar-
guerite Zentner. She was baptized by St. Leo's Catholic Church.

I remember Mom telling me how she never made many friends because she attended thirteen schools in twelve years. Although there's no way to be certain, I suspect her mother, who, according to her death certificate, died at age forty-eight of primary hemolytic jaundice, was alcoholic. Mom had never thought about her mother's sullen behavior until I told her the malt her mother guzzled might have contained alcohol.

"Well, she drank a lot of malt. She'd sit in her rocking chair with the shades drawn and drink one bottle after another," Mom said. "I had to bring it to her." Her voice trailed off as if she was back in that room with her mother instead of here with me. "I suppose that explains a lot."

Mom resented the fact that she had to change schools so often, each time because her mother wanted to start over in a new neighborhood. I never learned what she wanted to start over from, but I suspect it was what is referred to in recovery circles as a geographic cure. It will all be better in another place—until it isn't.

Prohibition ended in the U.S. in 1933, a year before Mom's mother died. That means she probably drank someone's home-brewed malt, so there's no telling what was in it. Mom's father, a druggist, might also have played a part in his wife's condition. All speculation. But what was clear was that Mom wanted out of what she described as a crazy household.

In 1932, soon after she turned nineteen, Mom married the man who rented a room in her parents' basement. Bob, a muscular but slender man with wavy black hair and an affable smile, seemed like a way into something better. Mom said she didn't marry for love but still made a good choice. Bob was a kind person and became a good husband.

"Bob used to wait on me hand and foot," Mom confided in me one day when her second husband Norm's demands had gotten the better of her.

Other than tidbits like that, Mom rarely talked about her early life with Bob. What I know is that in 1937, five years after they married, they had a child—a daughter named Marlee.

A sister I would never meet.

Mom, Bob, and Marlee lived in Detroit on the same street as Marlee's friend, Marcia. Marlee and Marcia were both toddlers when Mom, Bob, and Marlee moved first to a house around the corner and then eventually to a house down the block from Marcia's family. The girls became inseparable. The neighbors lived close in both contiguity and connection. They relied on each other to watch over the children and to help each other out when times grew difficult.

Marcia told me that she and Marlee were so close she called Marlee's parents Uncle Bob and Aunt Helen, and Marlee did the same with her folks. I couldn't help but think of the couple my brother and I embraced as our own, Uncle Norm and Aunt Betty, and began to appreciate the significance of what had become Marlee's extended family.

That family was put to the test, however, when Bob's promotion to supervisor at Michigan Bell required him to move his family from Detroit to Plymouth, a small town about forty-five minutes from their old neighborhood. It was there that tragedy turned their lives upside down.

Even though Marlee and Marcia didn't live on the same block anymore, they still got to see each other. Their parents made sure of that. But it meant they couldn't play together during the week.

Instead, Marcia's parents drove her to Plymouth on Saturday mornings so she could spend the day and sleep over that night. Mom and Bob would then drive Marcia back home the next day.

According to Marcia, it was on one of those sleepovers, in the summer of 1947, when they both woke up complaining of achiness and fever. Mom took their temperatures. Marcia had a low-grade fever, nothing too serious. But Marlee's fever was a different story.

"Bob, call the doctor," Mom shouted from the bedroom. "Marlee's fever's too high!"

The doctor told them to bring her in right away. When Bob picked Marlee up to take her to the car, she couldn't move her arms or legs. Panic rushed through them, but they tried not to think about what it might mean. Bob drove as fast as he could, while Mom clutched their moaning nine-year old daughter in her arms.

When the doctor examined Marlee, he didn't take long to come to a diagnosis. He saw Marlee's neck and back stiffness, her abnormal reflexes, her labored breathing, and heard her cries of pain. That was all he needed to speak the words that every parent back then dreaded to hear.

"She has polio."

Marlee never walked again.

People in the 1940s and early 1950's feared polio second only to the atomic bomb. Because polio disproportionately affected the young, parents isolated their children, especially in the warm summer months when the disease spread the fastest. Many parents prohibited their children from playing with friends, going to the movies, or swimming in the community pool for fear "the Crippler" would find them. The virus immobilized parents before it ever paralyzed their children.

For reasons Marcia doesn't understand, her parents weren't afraid of her catching polio from Marlee. Maybe it was because Marcia and Marlee were sleeping together the night Marlee got sick, and Marcia didn't get it. Maybe it was because Marcia's dad couldn't understand how people could let fear keep them from helping their friends.

"My father and mother had their own set of morals—what they thought was right," Marcia told me. "And what the neighbors did, not supporting and not coming out there, changed my father's opinion, and my mother's, about those people, how they felt about them. And in some way, I don't think they ever forgave them, if you want to know the truth."

I wondered if it was this same ironclad morality that eventually unraveled the relationship between her parents and Mom.

Marlee spent the first year of her illness in a hospital in Ann Arbor, twenty miles away from where they lived, in an isolated ward filled with other polio victims, most of them children like herself. As Marlee lay on her back, encased in a submarine-like device from the neck down, air pressure gradually increased against her chest and abdomen. When the pressure became intense enough, it slowly forced air out of her lungs. The vacuum created by her involuntary exhale drew air back into her lungs naturally. The air pressure in this negative-pressure ventilator, commonly referred to as an iron lung, squeezed it back out. Marcia told me that sometimes Marlee would stop—in mid-sentence—to wait for her breath to return.

When I heard Marcia describe what it was like to talk with Marlee this way, I tried to imagine the terror Mom and Bob felt seeing their daughter trapped in one of those mechanical beasts. I became obsessed with learning about iron lungs, how they worked, what they sounded like, and what it might feel like to be in one.

I discovered audio recordings of iron lungs online and listened over and over again to the haunting, Darth Vader-like sound, until I could hear it in my head without the recording. In. Out. In. Out. I went to see an old iron lung at a university library so I could wrap my arms around its girth, look through its porthole-like windows, and see Marlee's body in there as Mom must have. And as I lay in bed that night, I took in deep breaths and imagined the pressure of the iron lung forcing air out of me.

Each morning, Mom watched as the nurses unlatched the metal clasps that kept the iron lung's chamber airtight. She saw her daughter's body emerge from the big cylinder that surrounded her as they slid out the table on which Marlee lay. She had to witness them treat Marlee's arms and legs with compresses soaked in boiling water. The compresses smelled like an old wool coat drenched in rain, but she tried to ignore the smell because she knew the hot wraps loosened the muscles and allowed Marlee to relax. She wanted that for her. When the muscles became pliable, she watched the nurses stretch and massage her daughter's lifeless limbs. Mom suppressed the scream that battled to escape from deep inside her. She knew she had to steel herself against her daughter's pain to sustain the faith she so desperately needed in order to believe it was helping.

In my research about polio, I learned that many medical practitioners considered this approach radical and dangerous. Common medical practice at the time was to constrain polio victims' movement in splints and casts to protect the muscles from further damage. But that made no sense to Mom. She believed this new treatment would give Marlee a fighting chance to live.

"Sister Kenny really helped Marlee," Mom told me on one of the rare occasions when she talked about her illness. The way she spoke about Sister Kenny, as if she had been by Marlee's bedside the whole time, I thought she was one of the nuns at the hospital. Only later, when I learned more about polio, did I understand that Elizabeth Kenny, a self-trained nurse from the Australian bush-country, started a revolution in medical care with her in-novative treatment method. The Kenny Method, the foundation of what we now know as physical therapy, showed success where nothing else had. Sister Kenny's treatment became Mom and Bob's greatest hope.

But despite the intensive care, Marlee made little progress. When the doctors determined they had done all they could for her, they sent her home.

"To die," Marcia clarified. They brought her home to die? I imagined that bringing her home was a good sign, that she was getting better. I was sure Mom believed that, too. She would have hung on to every bit of hope and re-interpreted the slightest sign as the makings of a miracle.

Marlee's friends would come and stand outside the living room window to talk with her as she lay there day after day with an iron lung helping her breathe—keeping her alive breath by breath. Marcia said only the adults came, but Mom mentioned children coming, too. Their parents wouldn't let them go in—the adults wouldn't go in either—and they warned the kids about getting too close. Marlee could turn her head to face the window, but nothing more. Some of the kids would bring her Catholic medals and ask Mom to let Marlee know they were praying for her. Then they would run away as if the Crippler lay in wait behind the shrubbery. Mom hung those medals on the iron lung, praying that one of the saints would intercede for her and save her daughter. Those were the same medals Mom later made into a bracelet that she gave to Marcia, and Marcia, in turn, gave to me.

The more Marcia told me, the more I struggled with the enormity of what Mom and Bob must have endured to care for their daughter. Bob had to leave them to go to work every day. Mom was left to clean the house, cook the meals, and care for her crippled daughter. Nuns from the hospital came over to help move Marlee, clean her, and give Mom a few minutes of respite—even though they knew rest eluded her. Mom feared even leaving the room, Marcia told me. She worried something would happen and she wouldn't be there. That worrier side of Mom sounded all-too familiar, but in the years I knew her, nothing she worried about could have compared to those days with Marlee.

February 5, 1949, started out like a typical Michigan February day. The temperature was in the low teens. Clouds obscured the morning sun. Mounds of dirty snow framed the street. Marcia remembers what her parents told her about that day. She recalled it this way:

"I remember the night she died. She was being very...she was restless. She wasn't doing good that day. And Uncle Bob was, well, he went to pieces over it afterwards, my dad told me. Uncle Bob told Marlee she had to settle down because he had to go to work, and he needed some sleep. And I guess he was a little gruff. She went to sleep alright. For good. It just nearly killed him. It was awful."

Bob was not the same after Marlee died—Mom had told me that, and Marcia confirmed it. I could imagine that in Bob's mind his guilt for being gruff that night obliterated all the love and care he'd given her. Mom told me that in his grief, he repeatably banged his head against the brick of the house so hard that she had to take him to the hospital.

He sank into a depression so deep that he lost all interest in the outside world. He isolated himself from family and friends and created a life not much bigger than the iron lung that had imprisoned his beloved daughter. Mom struggled with managing her own grief—she had nothing left to manage his.

I felt the heat of the afternoon sun beating against my back as it made its way around my neighbor's house and through my study window. I pulled the blinds down partway to reduce the glare. It wasn't time yet to close them completely; I wanted to hold on to the last bit of daylight for as long as I could.

I had many more artifacts to examine—relics that related to the time after Marlee's tragic death. Grief hung heavy in the room. I needed to get out of this oppressive space, fill my lungs with air, and appreciate the gift of each exhale. As I stepped outside and took in the first deep breath since I'd started sorting hours before, scraps of other stories fought their way to the surface of my mind.

~

When I was a teenager, I remember my dad, Norm, saying to me, "I courted your mother through all her funerals." I never questioned it. I never thought about what a married man was doing courting a married woman, especially a Catholic man and a Catholic woman. I never asked what he meant by courting. I never asked about his wife, Aunt Betty, or about Mom's husband, Bob. By that time in my life, I was so used to not asking questions that they didn't even cross my mind. I didn't question the nuns about things that no longer made sense about my Catholic faith; I didn't question myself about why I wasn't like the other girls my age who couldn't talk about anything but boys; and I didn't question my parents about their earlier lives. I just smiled when Dad told me about his courting ritual and thought how bittersweet that sounded. Only as I remember it now do I wonder what he meant and regret not trying to find out more.

I don't know, for example, where Mom, Bob, Dad (Norm) and Betty first met. Chances are it was in the Marquis Toll House, the restaurant Dad and Betty owned. The restaurant catered to executives from Daisy Manufacturing Company (Dad's future employer), local business people from the downtown area, and the growing population of young working-class families such as Mom and Bob. Since they all attended Our Lady of Good Counsel, the only Catholic church in Plymouth, it's also possible they met there.

When Marlee died, Dad sent Mom and Bob flowers and attended the funeral. The next time they came into the restaurant, according to a story Dad shared with me, he refused to let them pay for their dinner. When Mom's father died two years later, Dad sent flowers again, and again made their next dinner on the house.

Then one more tragedy struck.

Four months pregnant with me and with a fifteen-month-old toddler in tow, Mom and Bob went to Dad's restaurant to enjoy a rare dinner out. While they were there, Bob collapsed. I don't know if Dad tried to resuscitate him or if he was the one who called the ambulance. It makes sense that he did, but this isn't a story he shared with me, so I don't know for sure.

What I do know from Mom is that the nearest hospital to the restaurant was eighteen miles away in Ann Arbor. By the time the ambulance arrived, Bob was gone. Mom probably knew there wasn't much hope. A couple of years earlier, about the time Jarrett was born, Bob was diagnosed with arteriosclerotic coronary artery disease. In the early 1950s, that was a death sentence. It was only a matter of time.

A 1952 newspaper clipping I discovered in Dad's things after he died offered me the first solid evidence that Dad and Bob knew each other before Jarrett was born. According to the article, they served together on the board of the newly formed Plymouth Republican Club—Dad as President and Bob as Secretary. That means that, if what Marcia told me was true, Dad and Bob volunteered together during the time Mom was pregnant with Jarrett (born August 1953). Did either of them know who the baby's father was? Did they both know? Were they such good friends that they made an agreement for Dad to father Bob's children, as Mom's friend Carolyn suggested? As much as I've struggled with it over the years and tried to put the pieces of this convoluted puzzle together, I've accepted the fact that I'll never have the answers to these questions.

Still, I wonder about the absurdity of Bob dying in Dad's restaurant. Did he know, or suspect, these two babies were not his, and if he did, did this affect his physical state enough to kill him? And how did his dying affect Mom's state of mind? Did she feel the same level of guilt Bob felt after Marlee's death? In the context of such a complex set of circumstances, who's to say they could even speak to each other about it? Was Mom's and Dad's eventual secret-keeping with Jarrett and me just an extension of the secrets they kept between themselves?

Whatever the true cause of Bob's death, for the third time in less than six years, Mom made funeral arrangements for a member of her immediate family. Dad sent Mom flowers and once again attended a funeral for a member of his friend's family.

All this tragedy put a different perspective on Mom's choices. Just like the bellows of the iron lung, with every inhale, came an exhale—bad news closely followed by good.

In 1953, the year Jarrett was born, Dr. Jonas Salk produced a polio vaccine. Though too late for Marlee, it was not too late for Jarrett and me. It took almost three years of testing for the vaccine to be declared safe and effective. On April 12, 1955, three weeks before, and only a couple of city blocks away from where I was born, Dr. Thomas Francis, from the University of Michigan's

School of Public Health, announced to a crowd of scientists, medical authorities and reporters, "The new Salk vaccine works, is safe, effective and potent."

People in the streets of Ann Arbor and around the world erupted in shouts of joy. Polio could now be prevented. I can only imagine that Mom breathed deeply for the first time in the seven years since Marlee got sick.

My sister was born into and died in a time of terror, while my brother and I were born into a time of hope. Parents no longer had to fear that their child would become "a polio." The grip that polio had on the lives of young families gave way to a breath of fresh air. Even though I was born without a father, I came into the world without the shadow of "the Crippler" looming over my every breath. I don't remember when I was vaccinated, but I know I was. I remember a nurse handing me a little sugar cube with medicine on it and telling me to put it in my mouth. I remember wishing all medicine tasted that good.

As the afternoon wore on, I found myself back where I'd started hours ago—surrounded by the scattered remnants of my family's past. The journey through these documents had been emotionally exhausting, leading me through the depths of my mother's grief and the complexities of my own origins. Now, with the setting sun casting long shadows across my study, it was time to bring order to this chaos of memories and put these pieces of the past to rest, at least for now.

I picked up each artifact, each official document, each clue that lay strewn across my study floor one last time and carefully slid it into a plastic sheet protector. I then added the page, in chronological order, to one of three three-ring binders: one for Mom, one for Norm, and one for me. As each document passed through my fingers, I found myself noting the nugget of evidence I extracted from it: the date and place of Mom's baptism, documentation of Mom and Bob's marriage, Norm and Bob's connection through the Plymouth Republican Club, the date and place of Mom and Norm's wedding, details of my adoption, and the fact that my birth certificate had been altered. I'd ferreted out as much truth as I could about my family's story from these last remaining relics of their lives. It was time to put them away.

As far as I could tell, I'd exhausted all the research avenues available to me. I closed each notebook and slid them into a storage box for another day. Although I didn't expect to find any more clues, certainly nothing of substance, I knew myself well enough to know that I would revisit all these documents again one day. They'd become like old friends who, even if we didn't see each other very often, provided an invaluable connection to a long-lost past I had no other access to.

I'd never know anything for sure. As frustrating as that was to me, I was gradually coming to accept that reality. What choice did I have?

What I didn't anticipate was that the advent of consumer-based genetic testing would soon change everything and the long sought after proof would be within my grasp.

CHAPTER TWENTY

Proof

A lthough consumer-based DNA testing has been around
since about 2012, and although I'm often an early-adopter
of new technology, I hadn't considered that it might be helpful to
me. I couldn't get DNA from my parents because they were both
already gone, so what good would it do me to take a test? When I
read an article about how DNA testing was helping adoptees find
their birth parents, even if they were deceased, by connecting them
to a family tree, I realized that I didn't need my parents DNA. I
could get some information even if I started with my brother.

My brother and I are so much alike—we're both techy, we share
a similar sense of humor, we like many of the same books, and, at
various points in our lives, we looked like we could be twins. As
a result, I never questioned whether we were full siblings. But all
this research got me thinking. What if we had different fathers?
What if Jarrett was Bob's son and I was Norm's? Because Bob died
before I was born, I have no photos or video of him with me, but

I do of him and Jarrett. That makes it easier to imagine. It would make sense if Mom decided to leave her husband and got pregnant once. But twice?

Jarrett and I were not that close as adults, partly because of a complicated relationship with his wife. After they separated, we grew closer, but what impact would it have on our burgeoning re-connection if we discovered we were only half siblings? The test wouldn't tell us who our biological fathers were. But, if it indicated we weren't full siblings, we could surmise that Bob was his and Norm was mine. It would move us a step closer to knowing something with scientific evidence.

I was nervous about asking him. I didn't know how he'd respond. I wasn't sure how much he wanted to know or what effect knowing this bit of the truth would have on his feelings about Norm. But I overcame my nervousness and called him.

"Sure," he said without any hesitation. "I'll do it."

So, in 2016, I ordered a test kit for him from 23andMe. I don't know why I bought it from there given I had an Ancestry account and had already been tested through them. I guess I figured 23andMe sounded more scientific, so he would respond more positively to it. In any event, it meant that to compare results easily, I would have to retest, too

I don't remember how long we waited for the tests to come back—a few weeks, a few months. It seemed like forever. Jarrett didn't care about having his own log-in. "You take care of that," he said.

"OK, I'll let you know what they say."

When I received the email that our results were in, I texted Jarrett. "There're back. "Do you want me to look or do you want to?"

"You go ahead," he replied. I couldn't tell if he was as nervous as me. As is his style, he didn't let on.

I took a deep breath, opened the email, and clicked the link. After I got through all the login and security screens, I saw a message, "You have new DNA relatives." I closed my eyes, said a quick prayer—I can't tell you for what—and clicked the link to take me there. It said:

Jarrett Marquis, Brother, 51.59% DNA Shared 45 Segments

Is that enough to be full siblings? I didn't even know. It made logical sense. I knew identical twins shared 100%, so wouldn't non-identical siblings share 50%? It didn't take me long to find out. The second Frequently Asked Question listed on the page told me what I needed to know: "What relationships are predicted by 23andMe?" Next to full sibling, it said 50% was the average % DNA shared, with an approximate range of 38%-61%.

I found my answer.

Jarrett and I were full siblings. We still didn't know if our father was Bob or Norm, but at least we could be positive it was the same person. A huge wave of relief spilled over me. I hadn't realized how much I wanted this to be true until I knew it was.

When I told Jarrett, he didn't act surprised. "I figured we were," he said, not showing much emotion—a reaction that didn't surprise me. "I don't know how it all happened, but I'm glad that's what you found out."

Me, too.

This experience inspired me to take the next step. What if I asked our cousin, David—Norm's closest living male relative, to take a test? If we were related to him in any way, it would prove that Norm was our dad. Otherwise, we wouldn't share any DNA. This would give us the definitive answer we were looking for. As Jarrett said, we'll never know how it all happened, but at least we'd know what happened.

David and I didn't see each other very often—maybe once every ten years or so, but when we were kids—very young kids—I imagined we'd get married. David was the only male I ever thought about marrying. We weren't related by blood, I reasoned, so it'd be OK. As adults we were Facebook friends, so that's how I reached out to him. Just like my brother, he said, "Sure" and just like my brother, he didn't care to access the results himself.

When the email arrived from 23andMe that the results were in, I found myself even more nervous than I was when I got Jarrett's. This was it. All the searching, all the wondering, all the digging for the truth could come down to this moment.

I laughed when I noted the date on the email, April 1, 2016. Whatever the result, this would go down in history as the biggest April Fools' Day joke ever. My mouse froze in my hand—the pointer hovering over the "view my reports" button in the email. I glanced out the window as dusk descended around me. Either I was a Marquis or was the child of a man I never met and never would. I closed my eyes, and as I did, my finger clicked the button. There was no going back now.

When I opened my eyes, I stared at the results. This time 23andMe listed two DNA relatives: a brother and a cousin. David and I were related. I now had irrefutable proof that Norm was my biological father—was our biological father. Everything I'd questioned, everything I'd imagined, everything I'd tried to understand came down to this. I'll never know how—DNA doesn't reveal the how—but I no longer have any room to doubt the truth.

I couldn't blame my parents for what they did—I knew how people, including myself, can find themselves in untenable situations. I didn't and still don't blame them for that. I do blame them, though, for what they did with it. Heat rose in my face. I could feel my muscles tensing, my jaw tightening. Jarrett and I deserved to know who our father was. And we deserved to know it from our parents.

My anger, however, quickly turned to grief. The corners of my eyes tightened, and tears started rolling down my cheeks. Maybe it had just gone on too long. Maybe it was Carolyn's touching attempt to preserve her friend's reputation. Maybe it was because I'd finally accepted the truth. Whatever the reason, I pressed my folded arms against my stomach and let my body convulse into tears. I cried for Marlee; I cried for Bob. I cried for my mother's grief, and for her torment at having to live a lie. I cried for Norm, the man who could never tell the children he loved so much that he was their father. But most of all, I cried for me. I cried for all the times I didn't cry, all the feelings I didn't let myself feel, and all the things I never knew because of my parents' secrets.

This piece of truth, the motivation behind what happened, I would never know, but I could no longer deny the fact that Norm was our father. For the first time in my life, I could feel Norm's blood coursing through my body, blood that carried genes that, among other things, made hair red.

When the tears subsided, I realized I could no longer ask for their apology or give them my forgiveness. They went to their graves with their pain—I could do nothing more for them. But I had a chance to live my own life free of the secrets that had permeated my earlier life. Perhaps this was the gift my parents gave me—clarity about the kind of person I'd become and the person I wanted to be, someone who admitted her mistakes, sought reconciliation, lived authentically, and stood up to injustice, even when, despite my mother's call for calm above all else, it made waves.

All the lies and secrets made me who I am and, although my hair's no longer red, I live with a fire that compels me to live life out in the open no matter what the cost. For that, I am grateful.

Chapter Twenty-One

Finally Legal, Finally Whole

Almost a year before the DNA test confirmed my parent-age, another momentous event occurred that would shape my journey toward living authentically. The date was June 26, 2015. On this day, the U.S. Supreme Court was expected to announce their decision in Obergefell v. Hodges, a case that could make marriage equality legal across the U.S. I'd set an alert on my phone, so I'd be notified as soon as it came through, but that didn't stop me from constantly checking.

Because of my position as LGBTQ and Multicultural Ministries Director for the Unitarian Universalist Association (UUA), it would be my job to announce the decision to the General Assembly, an annual meeting of thousands of Unitarian Universalists (UUs) from around the country and the world, this year being held in Portland, Oregon. I hoped I would have good news to share.

As I put down my phone for what felt like the fiftieth time so I could finish getting dressed, peaceful images and sweet smells of a serene botanical garden in Richmond, Virginia, from just eight months earlier flooded my mind.

On October 7, 2014, Wendy and I were legally married in a quiet ceremony in the garden. This followed the decision of the U.S. Supreme Court not to hear an appeal of the Fourth Circuit Court of Appeals' ruling in Bostic v. Schaefer, a ruling that made same-sex marriage legal in Virginia.

Over the previous ten years, a few other states had legalized same-sex marriage, but we'd decided, unlike many of our friends, that we would wait until we could marry in our home state. We didn't expect that would be anytime soon. When this ruling was allowed to stand, the day had come.

As soon as I heard the news, and before I could chicken out, I called Wendy at work—not something I often did, especially around lunch time. As a high school librarian, she usually had a library full of students and no time to talk. I thought she might make an exception for this call, though. When she picked up the phone, the impatience in her voice told me that I'd better get right to it, so I did.

"You wanna get married in the morning?" I asked with an impish lilt.

Her pause was palpable as she digested my out-of-the-blue question. The library sounds muted. I felt my heart skip a beat.

"Yes!" she said, her enthusiasm unmistakable. "Oh, my God! I can't believe it!" Her words spilled out in a rush as if she'd been holding her breath. "But I gotta go," she continued. I could hear students' animated voices rising in the background. "We'll talk when I get home." And with that, the line went dead.

I stared at the phone in my hand, my face reflecting back on the now black screen. The person I saw there was no longer a secretive, closeted young woman afraid of exposing herself to the world. Instead, I saw a confident, almost-60-year-old lesbian who refused to let others define her or be influenced by their judgements.

My parents taught me how to live in the closet by their example. Their secrets about Jarrett's and my parentage and the shame surrounding it instilled in me the feeling that I couldn't live my life in the open, that hiding my true self, especially those parts that others might object to, was a prerequisite to a happy, or at least safe, life.

But all that was behind me now. I could no longer keep my secrets, and I would no longer keep theirs. When I met Wendy in 2009, and we fell in love, all pretense was gone. She lived her life out in the open—at work, with her parents, her church community, and her extended family. Even if I was inclined to return to the closet, which I wasn't, we made a mutual decision to live our life as publicly as we could. Wendy has too much integrity to cover up who she is, and when we became a couple, we celebrated it with all who knew us, regardless of how they felt about our love.

Less than two years after meeting, we did what was unthinkable for most of my life—we held a church wedding. With the brief exception of sitting around a campfire at my friends' ceremony in Long Island so many years before where I imagined the two parts of me—the visible and the closeted—reuniting into one being who lived and loved openly, marriage, especially legal marriage, was never in my vision for myself. Why wish for something I couldn't have? But even more central was the question that had driven so much of my life: why stand out, why show people who I was in such a visible way, especially because I knew how much they might not like it?

Although I'd been out at work and in my public life for fifteen or more years at that point, standing and declaring my love in front of a church filled with people still seemed a step too far. All that changed when I met Wendy. I finally felt ready to take that next step, or, in this case, giant leap, into married life.

Our wedding represented so much more than the typical commitment ceremony. The 150 people in attendance included Wendy's family, her parents, brother, aunts, and cousins and the largest gathering of my family ever assembled, with my brother, nephews, nieces, and cousins on my mom's side who I hadn't seen in years. My work colleagues from as far away as Seattle and Wendy's from across town came to celebrate with us, and of course, several church friends from our Unitarian Universalist congregation where we held the wedding joined us.

The ceremony and reception that followed was a public statement that our love could not be denied by anyone, legally or not. It was an affirmation of the community that held us, and it was a call to them to help us survive the inevitable discrimination and prejudice we would experience in our lives together. In lieu of wedding presents, we asked guests to donate to Equality Virginia or the Gay Community Center of Richmond (Now Diversity Richmond) raising over $6,000 for these two organizations. We wanted to help make it possible for all people, not just us, to celebrate their love. Little did we know that four years later, the world would tilt on its axis, and marriage equality would be available to us in Virginia.

On the morning after my romantic lunchtime proposal, we approached the Henrico County Clerk's office to apply for a marriage license. We had no idea what to expect. We arrived before they opened and waited in the parking lot for a few minutes before excitement and nervousness got the better of us. Surprised to find the county administration building open and people already passing through security, we took our place in line. No one entering looked like a gay or lesbian couple on a similar mission. We were the first and only. At least as far as we could tell.

As we reached the clerk's office on the second floor, Wendy and I looked at each other and smiled lovingly before Wendy pulled the door open.

"We're here to apply for a marriage license," one of us—I don't remember which one—said to the woman behind the counter.

"Fill out those forms," she replied, pointing to a table with pink and blue forms secured on various colored clipboards. "It doesn't matter which one you complete. Either color will work," she added. I could see the smirk on Wendy's face and feel one on my own.

Being the butchier of the two of us, and because I've never liked pink, I picked up a clipboard with a blue form. Wendy, who loves pink, gravitated to that one.

The office had gotten a little busier in the few minutes it took us to complete the forms, so as we approached the counter again, this time with forms in hand, we waited behind someone dressed in a suit, probably an attorney. When he completed his business, we handed our pink and blue forms to the clerk. She accepted them without a smile, and I wondered how she felt about this new wrinkle to her work, specifically, how she felt about same-sex couples getting married. I couldn't help it. I'd spent a lifetime wondering how people perceived me—judged me—and just because I lived my life out in the open now, didn't mean that worry had disappeared.

For the next several minutes, we waited while she attempted, with wrinkled brow and pursed lips, to plug our information into their computer system. Two other women hovered over her shoulder, watching her every keystroke. Perceiving our apprehension, one of them attempted to reassure us, "The computers haven't been updated yet, and we have to cover for her when she goes to lunch, so we have to know what to do."

We nodded. So maybe the stress-filled faces were just that—people trying to figure out how to do their jobs now that they were being asked to do something new. That's what I wanted to believe.

When the clerk finally handed us our license, she didn't say congratulations. In fact, she didn't say anything. Wendy took the license and we turned to leave—Wendy to her left toward the door we came in and me, for some unexplained reason, to my right. As I approached the door in front of me and reached for the handle, I stopped short. Printed in bold letters at about eye level were the words, "CLOSET" and beneath that "DO NOT ENTER." Without skipping a beat, I said, apparently loudly enough that others heard, "Whoops, wrong door. I just came out of there."

People burst out laughing. From the resolute businesspeople in line to the harried clerks behind the counter, people laughed. We did, too. The tension that permeated the room just moments before broke apart as if a glitter bomb had exploded above us and rained down on everyone.

We left the building still laughing, our eyes wet, knowing that on their first full day of granting same-sex marriage licenses in Virginia, the staff at the clerk's office would have a story to tell around the dinner table that night.

"That's going to be something they'll remember," one man shouted across the parking lot as he waved at us.

I was glad to bring other people joy on our joyous day.

An hour later, our simple ceremony in the botanical garden, with six dear friends as witnesses, one of them on an iPad, lasted a total of six minutes. It was as if our church wedding from four years earlier had been interrupted and now, we were finally finishing it. Except this time, when we kissed, we were legally married in the eyes of the Commonwealth of Virginia.

Even as I remembered those moments while brushing my hair in a hotel room on the opposite side of the country, I couldn't imagine that same-sex marriage might become legal nationwide less than a year later.

Just as I finished getting ready, my phone buzzed and the message I'd been waiting for flashed across my screen: "The U.S. Supreme Court has ruled in favor of same-sex marriage." As I read the news, my knees buckled and I reached for the support of the bed behind me. My hands shook as I announced the news to Wendy, "They did it! The Court ruled in favor of marriage!"

She ran across the room, sat down next to me, and we hugged for what seemed like an eternity, tears running down our faces. When we finally released each other, I said, "I've gotta get moving. I've got to plan how to make the announcement to the General Assembly."

Two hours later, surrounded by as many same-sex couples as we could get on stage, I stood in front of a crowd of thousands of UUs, and read from Justice Kennedy's majority opinion.

> No union is more profound than marriage, for it embodies the highest ideals of love, fidelity, devotion, sacrifice, and family. In forming a marital union, two people become something greater than once they were. As some of the petitioners in these cases demonstrate, marriage embodies a love that may endure even past death. It would misunderstand these men and women to say they disrespect the idea of marriage. Their plea is that they do respect it, respect it so deeply that they seek to find its fulfillment for themselves. Their hope is not to be condemned to live in loneliness, excluded from one of civilization's oldest institutions. They ask for equal dignity in the eyes of the law. The Constitution grants them that right.

The crowd roared. Wendy and I hugged and cried again, as did the many couples on stage with us. Our dream, the dreams of so many LGBTQ+ people across America had been fulfilled. We were free to love and marry just like heterosexual couples had for centuries. And even though, in some states, we could still lose our jobs, be denied housing, and barred from adopting children, from this day forward, no one could deny us the right to marry the person we loved.

Unitarian Universalist General Assembly, Portland, OR, reacting to the news
(Nancy Pierce Photo)

As I stood on the stage with hundreds of cameras focused on me, I felt like I'd reached the culmination of my own journey to openness and integrity. Although it would be another year before I opened the DNA results that proved that Norm was my biological father, I knew at that moment—on that stage—that I'd left all my secrets behind. I felt whole for the first time in my life.

Epilogue

My parents made choices that I will never understand, just as I lived a life they couldn't understand or accept. Their choices weighed heavily on how I lived my life, but that doesn't change the fact that I loved them and always knew they loved me. Would they have been happy at news of my marriage? Would they have attended our wedding? I can't know. I hold out hope that Mom would have evolved as marriage equality became more acceptable in our society. She feared being judged more than she feared doing the wrong thing. The Supreme Court decision would have influenced her stance—I'm certain of that.

Friends have asked me if I forgive my parents for lying to me, especially about something as consequential as my parentage. I can say unequivocally that just as I said, "I do" to my marriage, I can say, "I do," to that question. Love is not perfect, just as we are not perfect. I have made my share of mistakes too, and I hope I can be forgiven for them.

What I've learned is that my life is so much better when I live it in wholeness and truth. I've come to accept that holding on to anger, resentment, and distrust impacts me as much, if not more than it does the other person. I would give anything to sit down and have a conversation with Mom and Dad, to let them know that I forgive them and, hopefully, free them from some of the guilt that burdened them. Instead, all I can do is write the story—my story—and let anyone who reads this know I am happy and whole in spite of and, maybe because of, the lies they told.

According to Newton's Third Law of Motion, for every action, there is an equal and opposite reaction. Singer/songwriter John Hartford of "Gentle on my Mind" fame, wrote a song called "I Would Not Be Here." The first couple lines, "I would not be here if I hadn't been there, And I wouldn't been there if I hadn't just turned," sum up the way I've lived my life, knowing that every decision, including mistakes, leads us to the next thing and the next thing and the next thing. For every action, there is an equal and opposite reaction.

If Marlee hadn't died, I wouldn't have been born. If Bob hadn't died, maybe I would have learned the truth sooner. If my parents hadn't lied, who knows how my life would have been different, how I would have been different? If I'd come out and stayed out as the proud lesbian I am now, maybe Mom would have found a way to accept me while she was still alive. I'll never know because that didn't happen. What happened shaped my life, and I'm grateful for every scar, every triumph, every lie, and every truth because they've all made me who I am. And I'm pretty proud of that.

Acknowledgements

I never had any intention of writing a memoir. However, I entered the Solstice MFA program in Creative Writing in 2011 because after years of technical writing, I knew I needed help in expressing my ideas in more engaging ways than writing about software allowed. As I sat at the lunch table one day, I listened to the program's extraordinary director, Meg Kearney, and other students in the program share their adoption stories. At a lull in the conversation, I mentioned that I'd a rather unique twist on an adoption story. Eager to hear yet another tale of the impact of being raised by adoptive parents, I proceeded to tell them that the man who adopted me was, in fact, my biological father. I watched as forks hung in midair and heads tilted to the side while people tried to process what I was telling them.

"Yeah," I went on, "my parents never told us that he was our biological father." I proceeded to relate the short version of the story that you read in its complete form here.

"You have to write that!" Ann Breidenbach insisted. As others chimed in their agreement, I decided that I needed to consider their exuberant reactions. So, write it, I did, even though it would eventually take me thirteen years. Thank you, Ann and Meg, for your encouragement.

The first version, which I submitted as my creative thesis for my MFA program, felt like a collection of stories that had some relationship to each other, but had only begun to reveal the truths I was learning about my parents and myself. I couldn't have gotten anywhere near that far, however, without support from my other nonfiction classmates, especially Kassie Rubico, Rich Tombeno, and Beth Richards.

Most of the credit, however, for molding my writing into something worth reading goes to teacher/author-extraordinaire, Anne-Marie Oomen. Her patient and insightful feedback helped me craft the early versions of this story. Her unwavering support of my work gave me the courage to revisit it (and revisit it and revisit it) until I landed on the words and story contained here. Fittingly, I wrote the last chapter of this memoir at the Solstice Alumni writing retreat in 2024. It felt like coming home in the deepest meaning of that expression.

When I decided to independently publish this book, I relied on the support of an incredible writing community, James River Writers (JRW), to figure out what I knew, what I had to learn, and everything in between. I especially want to thank JRW's Executive Director, Katharine Herndon, for her encouragement and resources, author Bill Blume, for pointing me to Atticus to design the book's interior, and the incomparable illustrator/designer/author Phill Hilliker, for turning my draft into a beautiful cover.

Thirteen years after sitting at that lunch table with my Solstice family, I began the seven-month journey of publishing this manuscript in serialized form on Substack (Annette's Wanderings). The comments I received there from people I consider to be my beta readers gave me invaluable feedback, inspired me to keep publishing, and helped me develop the courage to put this story out into the world. Thank you, Lisa, Nan, Denise, Gloria, Jerry, Kate, Barbara, Kathleen, Roxanne, Julie, and everyone else who took the time to comment on a chapter (or more). Your support has been invaluable!

I want to extend a special thank-you to Troy Ford, a person I met on Substack and am now happy to call a friend. Troy took it upon himself to gather all the LGBTQ-related content of Substack under one umbrella he named Q-Stack: The LGBTQIA+ Directory of Substacks. This invaluable resource is a gift in and of itself. But in addition, Troy's been amazingly generous with his comments, encouragement, and shout-outs. I can't thank you enough, Troy! You've made the Substack journey a much less lonely one.

I also want to thank my family. Specifically, I want to thank my brother Jarrett, who willingly agreed to take a DNA test, and then when I asked his permission to use photos of him in my book, he replied with an enthusiastic, "Yes! Use whatever photos you'd like." Thank you, Jarrett, for all your support and love.

I also want to thank my cousin, David, who also responded graciously when I asked him for his DNA. Without his generosity, Jarrett and I would never have been able to prove our lineage. I am eternally grateful.

Finally, I can't even begin to express my gratitude for my wife Wendy. She not only supported me emotionally through these many years of crafting this story but served as my developmental/copy editor and proofreader (although, let me be clear, I take full responsibility for any errors or typos in this book!). Her own writing (which you can sample on her Substack, Furrow and Fire), inspires me, and, if I'm honest, makes me envious at times. She is a dedicated professional, a beautiful writer/poet, and a loving and giving partner. Thank you, Wendy, for your love, your compassion, and your unbounded support of my work and of me.

It takes a village!

ABOUT THE AUTHOR

Annette Marquis would love to say that writing is her only passion but, truth be told, she has so many passions that writing has to fall in line with all the rest. First and foremost, she's a lesbian feminist committed to justice and equity for all people. Her activism is fueled by her conviction that all people deserve to be treated with dignity and respect.

Annette has a Master of Social Work degree from Boston University that she applied to a twenty-five-year career in chemical dependency treatment and mental health crisis intervention services. She is a founding member of Allies for Racial Equity, The Pledge to End Racism, and The Living Legacy Project. More recently, she received a Master of Fine Arts degree in Creative Nonfiction from the Solstice MFA in Creative Writing Program, now associated with Lasell University in Newton, MA.

Over the years, Annette has co-authored over twenty-five books on Microsoft software and computing, contributed to multiple anthologies, and published three memoirs, *Resistance: A Memoir of Civil Disobedience in Maricopa County*, *Accidental Mentors: Inspirational Stories of Women Who Shaped My Life by Just Being Themselves* (serialized on Substack and coming soon in other formats) and *Living Into the Truth, A Daughter's Journey of Discovery*.

Annette spends her discretionary time enjoying travel, gardening, bird watching, hiking, photography, and following women's basketball, sometimes alone, but preferably, with her wife, Wendy. Since 2010, her home base has been Richmond, Virginia.

Also by Annette Marquis

Coming soon in
print and eBook
formats

Completely revised
2nd ed. coming soon

Subscribe to Annette's newsletter

www.wordswomen.com

www.ingramcontent.com/pod-product-compliance
Lightning Source LLC
Chambersburg PA
CBHW020231130626
46549CB00005B/1835